THE WINDMILL TURNING

THE WINDMILL TURNING

Nursery Rhymes, Maxims, and
Other Expressions of Western
Canadian Mennonites

VICTOR CARL FRIESEN

 THE UNIVERSITY OF ALBERTA PRESS

First published by
The University of Alberta Press
Athabasca Hall
Edmonton, Alberta, Canada
T6G 2E8
1988

Translation of verses and commentary upon them copyright © Victor
Carl Friesen 1988
Copyright this edition © The University of Alberta Press 1988

ISBN 0-88864-118-4 cloth

Canadian Cataloguing in Publication Data

Friesen, Victor Carl.
   The windmill turning

   Bibliography: p.
   Includes index.

   1. Mennonites - Canada - Folklore. 2.
   Mennonites - Canada - History. 3. Folk
   literature, Low German - Canada. I. Title.
   GR113.7.M45F75 1988   398.2 04394   C86-091465-8

55,826

Typesetting by The Typeworks, Vancouver, British Columbia, Canada
Printed by D. W. Friesen & Sons Ltd., Altona, Manitoba, Canada

 FOR

MOTHER

The forebears of Western Canadian Mennonites came originally from the Netherlands, where stately windmills graced the skyline. In their treks across Europe—to Poland and to Russia—and finally on to America, these Mennonites continued to build windmills to drain marshlands and grind grain. Today at the Mennonite Village Museum in Steinbach, Manitoba, a four-storey mill is the centre attraction. Its huge sails turn in a gentle wind as countless other sails have turned on other mills throughout the past four-and-a-half centuries of Mennonite history. Always a people struggling to survive against adversity, verbalizing their day-to-day life in homely folklore, always the windmill turning. . . .

CONTENTS

FOREWORD

In Canada we live in a society that not only cherishes ethnic identities but seeks to preserve and support them in various ways. "Vive la difference!" might be our ethnic watchword. And yet, there are always subtle counterforces in a pluralistic society such as ours that push ethnic groups the other way, towards assimilation and homogeneity. It is one of the ironies of social history that full ethnic self-awareness characteristically comes to an ethnic group after the fact, so to speak, as glimpses in a rearview mirror caught as the ethnic experience is already receding swiftly behind it.

So it is with the Mennonites. For hundreds of years this ethno-religious group lived in isolated communities in various northern and eastern European countries—the Netherlands, West Prussia (Danzig area), Poland and Russia—where they cultivated their own religious and ethnic identity, their own language and culture. Their ethnic language was *Plautdietsch*, a West Prussian dialect which became the warp and woof of Mennonite ethnic identity. Today the Mennonites of Canada are largely assimilated culturally and linguistically, although most still cling to their Anabaptist religious beliefs and to at least some of their traditional ethnic folkways. *Plautdietsch*, however, is disappearing rapidly as a daily language, and the memory of what it felt like to live a life of total immersion as ethnic Mennonites is fading along with it. And that is where the rearview mirror comes in. Now that most Mennonites are living within mainstream Canadian society, they are developing a more sophisticated awareness of their traditional folkways and ethnic language and the unique perspectives they offer.

The result, as Victor Carl Friesen observes in his Introduction, is that Canadian-Mennonite communities are experiencing a flurry of literary and artistic activity which celebrates an ethnic language and culture that may well be facing ultimate extinction. A central focus of the Low German literary revival at the moment are the superb writings a generation ago of Arnold Dyck. Literature in *Plautdietsch* began with Dyck, and all subsequent writing in that language is heavily in his debt. A major literary figure by any standard, Dyck wrote Low German comic novels, plays and short stories which had they been written in English would have placed him among Canada's finest humorists, including that other humorist of Mennonite extraction—Paul Hiebert.

Arnold Dyck's melancholy prediction was that the rich Russian-Canadian-Mennonite ethnic heritage he wrote about would soon be lost if *Plautdietsch* ceased to be the everyday language of Canadian Mennonites. He was right in foreseeing that assimilation would inevitably lead to the demise of Low German, but what he failed to anticipate was that with assimilation would come a new generation of culturally advanced Mennonites dedicated to keeping alive their ethnic language, at least in a literary form. At the same time Mennonite literary artists like Rudy Wiebe, Patrick Friesen and Sandra Birdsell, among others, were writing about their Mennonite ethnic experience for a much wider non-Mennonite readership, thus preserving and popularizing it in yet a new form and language.

This brings me to Victor Carl Friesen's fascinating collection of Mennonite folklore as presented here. These traditional nursery rhymes, proverbs and maxims represent, one might say, the kitchen middens of Mennonite ethnic culture. What this collection reveals about Mennonite life experience in *Plautdietsch* is as authentic and significant in its way as the literary myths presented in poetry, fiction and drama. These miniature gems of Mennonite folklore form coruscating patterns of feelings, attitudes and folk wisdom in their own right. Like folk songs and fairy tales they represent ordinary experience carved and polished into timeless forms that seem both spontaneously generated and at the same time artfully wrought by some superior artistic faculty.

And what do these scores of verses, songs and sayings tell us about the Mennonite mind and heart? Those who know the history of this sober, pious but practical-minded Anabaptist sect, once savagely persecuted for its beliefs but always stubbornly clinging to its isolated way of life as "the silent in the land," may be surprised to find innocent light-heartedness, a sense of fun, playful wit and sheer frivolity of expression in so much of the material. But even the devout, strait-laced Mennonites could not live by the Bible alone. The human urge to play—*homo ludens*—especially verbal play, is an irresistible characteristic of children of all ages. Like any peasant people living close to the land, the Mennonites of Europe satisfied their urge to play with language by making up nonsense verses, light-hearted songs and pithy sayings about the simple elemental world around them. Nature, animals, human appetites—including the more voracious ones—the significant stages of the hu-

man cycle—birth and innocence, youth and love, marriage and parenthood, old age and death—were the stuff the creative folk instinct worked on. Whimsy, fantasy and nonsense were given free reign along with serious insights, realistic fears and hopes, and mordant strokes of wit. Regard, for example, the sexual playfulness of "Patch on hole/ You take I still," or the wry humor of "There are people, turtles and three-cornered files" [in this strange world].

Dr. Friesen has not only gathered a large, variegated body of folklore, but has organized it in a clear, effective manner by starting with the "songs of innocence" of nursery rhymes and children's songs and games and then proceeding to the various categories of adult maxims and proverbs. And he has considerately provided two translations for each item—one literal and unretouched, the second more polished and "poetic." There are a few places where one might wish for an amalgamation of the two, but by and large this method allows Dr. Friesen to combine accurate meaning with graceful poetic form in his translations. He also provides a helpful historical survey of the Mennonites and of *Plautdietsch*, their traditional language of hearth and home.

Dr. Friesen has tried to solve the difficult problem of an acceptable orthography for *Plautdietsch* with tact, good sense and a commendable degree of accommodation and compromise. The problem of "fixing" the spelling of a language that was spoken for centuries but not written is not so easily overcome. No orthography can be completely phonetic, indeed the very concept of a "phonetic" language is one of those illusions we pretend to regard as a reality. A case in point is the "tj" versus "kj" controversy in *Plautdietsch*. In plain fact both symbols are simply agreed-upon conventions. Neither is more "phonetic" than the other, and Low German speakers in reality make exactly the same sound whether they "think" "tj" or "kj."

Folklore of all kinds is enjoying great popularity in our time, and there is much in this collection that should appeal to non-Mennonite readers as well as Mennonite readers. The inner facets of the Mennonite psyche are colorfully on display here and the collective consciousness of one group can throw interesting light on the consciousness of other groups. It is my personal hope that Mennonite mothers of today will be inspired enough by this fine collection to teach their children some of the rhymes and games in it (the instructions are quite adequate) in *Plautdietsch*, or at least in the translated versions.

Victor Carl Friesen has made a valuable and unique contribution to Mennonite folklore.

Al Reimer
University of Winnipeg

ACKNOWLEDGMENTS

I wish particularly to acknowledge my debt to Gerhard Lohrenz's *The Mennonites of Western Canada*, 1974, for providing an insightful, judicious overview of Mennonite history. It was the background knowledge gained from this booklet which gave focus to much of my research for Part I of this book. C. Henry Smith's *The Story of the Mennonite People*, 1981, and, of course, *The Mennonite Encyclopedia*, 4 vols., 1955–59, supplied much detailed information. For a more homely description of Mennonite culture, I was pleased to be able to consult Julius G. Toews and Lawrence Klippenstein, eds., *Manitoba Mennonite Memories*, 1974. Two of the scholarly articles in this collection, by Mr. Frank Harder and by Dr. H. Leonard Sawatzky, were valuable sources of information, and separate references to them are found in the footnotes—as there are to several other invaluable studies, too numerous to name here (a bibliography for "Further Reading," with full citations, is found at the end of my book). However, Herman Rempel's *Kjenn Jie Noch Plautdietsch? A Mennonite Low German Dictionary*, 1984, deserves special mention. Although I had completed the first draft of my manuscript before it became available to me, Rempel's book was put to one of the prime uses of any dictionary—to check the spelling in my own writing of *Plautdietsch* in Part II.

Several people gave individual help and encouragement. Dr. Lawrence Klippenstein, Historian-Archivist, Mennonite Heritage Centre, Winnipeg, most obligingly answered all my queries and provided other information. Dr. Jack Thiessen, Department of German, University of Winnipeg, critically read through the manuscript, offered useful suggestions, and shared with me some of the findings of his own research. Another University of Winnipeg professor, Dr. Al Reimer, Department of English, was painstaking in his reading of the manuscript, bringing to bear his wide knowledge of Mennonite history and culture. Mary Mahoney-Robson, again as with a previous book of mine, gave expert editorial assistance.

I am also grateful to those various people who took an interest in my work and recalled for me some item of folklore I had not previously recorded in my ten or so years of collecting. For my mother, Anna Friesen, aged 88, who has an ear for these bits of folklore, I reserve my deepest thanks. Without her, the book would not have taken shape. I am grateful that just as she was able to learn so many rhymes and maxims from her parents, so I was able to learn them from her.

I was pleased to have Wendy Kershaw illustrate the folklore items. Her pen-and-ink drawings do much to enhance their presentation.

 PART ONE

Western Canadian Mennonites

Introduction

Since the time of the Mennonites' first arrival in Western Canada, several misconceptions have arisen about these people, their language and customs. Understandably so, for the term "Mennonite" itself can refer to a religious affiliation and/or an ethnic group. (A present-day Vietnamese refugee, harbored by a Mennonite family, might choose to become a Mennonite in religion but could certainly not say he had a Mennonite heritage.) Then, too, in the course of their 450-year-old history, the Mennonites have trekked from country to country, several times over (the earlier treks at a time when national boundaries as we understand them today had little meaning), so that to some they appeared to be representative of whatever larger culture in which they had at one time lived.

As well, Western Canadian Mennonites fostered some of the confusion about their identity. They either were too diffident in acquiescing to surmises made by others (a fairly typical immigrant attitude) or were too assertive in emphasizing one part of their rich heritage to the exclusion of other aspects. Some of the terminology which pertains to the Mennonites is itself misleading—the term, "Low German," for instance—unless one understands its origin. And Mennonites perhaps have been lax in not clearing up these matters.

The result has been that misconceptions in the public mind concerning these Mennonites are still prevalent today. That they be explained may eventually become just an academic concern since the Mennonites have already more or less merged with the rest of Canadian society. But in a book such as this, devoted to the folklore of these people, it makes sense to have a broad understanding of their heritage.

ONE

A Unique History

The unique history of the Mennonites who emigrated from Europe to Western Canada (and the American Midwest) in 1874 and the years that followed did much to shape their rich folklore which is the focus of this book.

These people came originally from the Netherlands area in the sixteenth century and were of hardy Flemish and Frisian stock. In fact, it was these same people who, centuries before at the time of Christ, had so stoutly resisted Julius Caesar and his Roman Legions in his conquest of Europe. They were very jealous of their home-*land*, wrung with much labor from the marshy Dutch coast, and would not give it up easily to any usurper. "Rather dead, than slave" was their motto. The Romans called them *Frisii*, meaning "frizzled-haired." During Charlemagne's later reign the whole Netherlands region was simply denominated "Friesen" (cf. the present-day province there of Friesland, the Frisian Islands, and Holstein-Friesian cows). Among today's Mennonites in Western Canada, "Friesen," with it geographical derivation, is probably the most common surname. In many Mennonite communities one can readily name a dozen Friesen families, none of which is related to any of the others.

Five centuries after Caesar's time, people from the lowlands became migrants—more particularly those lowlanders farther east along the coastline from Emden to Denmark but which still, broadly speaking, included part of Frisia.[1] There they had prospered enough to require more land holdings (only so much could be done in dredging up mounds in swamps) and thus began the migration across the English Channel to Britain. This was the so-called Anglo-Saxon invasion, but these were not always war-like people. Southeast England in those days was largely swampy too, and these people who had left the continental lowlands were soon comfortably settled, living their homely rural lives and continuing the British pastoral tradition. (It is unfortunate that the acronym WASP was ever coined, for its haughty connotation is not characteristic of Anglo-Saxon down-to-earthness but rather of the courtly Norman pretensions which held sway after William the Conqueror's takeover in 1066. Both Sir Walter Scott and Charles Kingsley make much of the differences in Anglo-Saxon and Norman outlook in their respective novels, *Ivanhoe*, 1819, and *Hereward the Wake*, 1866.)

Let a millenium pass since the departure of some lowlanders to Britain, and we come to the beginnings of

5

Mennonitism back on the continent in 1525. The religion was part of the Reformation sweeping through Europe then which spawned such breakaway church groups as the Lutherans and the Calvinists. The Mennonites were more radical yet and so gained the enmity of other Protestant faiths as well as Catholicism.

Whereas these groups still believed in a central religious authority, albeit not from Rome, the Mennonites did not. The printing press had made the Bible available to everyone, and it alone, together with one's individual conscience in following its precepts, was all the authority needed, they thought. Mennonite followers would be adults acting voluntarily to live a life of sanctification, to translate faith into deeds. Thus there could be no infant baptism, only a simple form thereof among free, mature individuals.

This latter practice earned for the Mennonites the disparaging label "Anabaptists" (re-baptizers), but that was the least of their troubles. Their stand against religious authority at a time when church and state worked hand in glove had its political implications which appeared to threaten the position of all ruling classes. The Mennonite refusal to go to war lessened the might of grasping lords who, when they were not engaging in conflict for their own imperialistic ends, hired out mercenaries for diplomatic or monetary gain. As well, the Mennonite refusal to swear oaths or to hold public office seemed to be a slap in the face to government officials. The result was that the Anabaptists were considered true revolutionaries, a menace to church and state, to be systematically hunted down and killed.

And killed they were, burned at the stake, beheaded, or drowned—several thousands of them. One authority has stated that no denomination (excluding the Hutterites) had so many martyrs.[2] An early account of the persecution, Tieleman Jansz van Braght's *Martyrs Mirror*, published in the Netherlands in 1660, has become a significant document in Mennonite literature. Most of the deaths had occurred among Swiss Anabaptists, and

that in the first ten years of the group's existence, for it was these people who had given rise to the movement. But about two thousand deaths also occurred in the Netherlands. The Dutch adherents were following the maxim of their long-ago ancestors in choosing to die rather than be slave to ideas which they could not accept with free conscience.

Whereas the great purge had the effect of curtailing Anabaptism elsewhere, the movement could not be so easily quelled in the Netherlands. This country was entering a period of expansive activity—world exploration and colonization, robust trade and industry, advances in medicine and science, and growth in the arts (the superb landscape artist, Jacob van Ruysdael, was a Mennonite, and even Rembrandt, if not a Mennonite, was at least one with strong sympathies towards this religion).

The Dutch mentality was open to new ideas, particularly those stressing freedom and individualism, and one Menno Simons, a Dutch priest from the province of Friesland, joined the Anabaptist movement in 1536, eleven years after its founding in Switzerland. Thus, the man who was to give his name to the group did not initiate the church as, say, Martin Luther did the Lutheran Church. Instead, his leadership and scholarly work (he wrote twenty-five books) made him in time a dominant member. For part of his life he had to flee from place to place while fulfilling his ministerial role, for there was a price on his head. However, he was able to die a natural death as some aristocrats became more tolerant of Anabaptist beliefs.

Meanwhile, Menno Simons's fellow believers and countrymen fled too, if they could, in order to live according to the dictates of their consciences. These were the men and women who would be the forebears of the Mennonites eventually settling in Western Canada. They were fortunate in finding sanctuary under the wing of some Polish Catholic noblemen who placed more importance on the people's marsh-draining and dyke-building expertise than on their Protestant faith.

The farmyard of the great-grandparents of the author at Mountain Lake, Minnesota. The combined house and barn was typical of Mennonite farms in Russia and in the early years in North America. Note the wash drying on the hedge.

The sanctuary was the delta of the Vistula River, the environs of what is now Gdansk (then called Danzig). In 1530 when the first Dutch refugees arrived, the area was pure swamp so that, although they had escaped religious persecution, they had not found a Garden of Eden. They would make it nearly so in the course of four or five generations, but at what terrible cost! One report says that eighty per cent of the Mennonites fell victim to swamp fever.[3]

Conquering such terrain, however, was part of the age-old heritage. The Frisians had survived as a people in Roman times, and men of their own blood had settled the fenlands of Britain. No wonder that Hereward the Wake had put up such a stalwart resistance against the Normans when he had recourse to his marshy hideout at Ely in East Anglia. They were all lowlander "frogs" or "toads," a sobriquet sometimes applied to them by others in previous homelands—in Friesland or Great Britain. Now in Poland they had to be "toads" again (*Kjräte* in their own language). Interestingly enough,

this term *Kjräte* is still an epithet among our Mennonites, even if they are living in an arid climate, in mid-continent, on the Canadian or American prairies—but it is used only in a derogatory way with individuals, never in a collective sense regarding themselves.

There was one notable area in America in modern times where Mennonites were called upon to practise their ancient art of draining farmland. My mother's people, who chose to settle at Mountain Lake, Minnesota, when their fellow Mennonites were first settling in Manitoba in 1874–75, had to underlay their land with a network of tiles or pottery pipes for drainage purposes before it could produce the fine crops of corn and soybeans which it does today. The original lake for which the community was named was also drained and produces at the time of this writing a harvest of sugar cane, of all things—perhaps one of only a few such crops in the northern States!

In the Vistula delta in the sixteenth and first half of the seventeenth centuries, the Mennonites secured individual farms by digging drainage ditches and using the dredged-up earth, piled into mounds, for their farmyards. Space was at a premium, and the Old Country style of having house and barn connected under one roof seemed more practical than ever. Mennonites built them at right angles to each other. Planted trees and shrubs about the yard helped to prevent water erosion, and with time and hard work the holding would be increased in size. Windmills, as in the Netherlands, dotted the landscape, for they provided the power to pump water from the low-lying land.

The Mennonites in question lived in this area for two-and-a-half centuries. It was here that they were becoming an ethnic group, surrounded as they were by non-Dutch people. Although they thought of themselves as Dutch throughout this time and retained close ties with the Netherlands, their isolation and common hardships added to their feeling of being a distinct cultural identity.

This identity was borne home to them all the more because of the restrictions imposed on them from without. There was religious tolerance, yes, but the native Poles did not want to lose any of their own people to the Mennonite faith. There could be no proselytizing by the Mennonites, not even the construction of a church building for their own members—until 1768 (they could, however, hold their own services with their own ministers and operate their separate schools). Furthermore, if there were to be any intermarriages, so the restrictions ran, then the Mennonite partner would automatically lose his or her Mennonite status. Only children of *two* Mennonite parents could join their church when they became adults.

In one sense the Mennonites were not unhappy with these restrictions. Their community in time still prospered and grew—what with its emphasis on day-to-day hard labor and an emphasis on cohesive family life. The Mennonites could live their separate lives, aloof from their non-Dutch neighbors, and feel that their simple lives would not be tainted or corrupted by outside influences. One effect of such an existence was that the group throughout its two-and-a-half century stay on the Vistula maintained the original gene-pool dating from its Dutch origin.[4]

When, almost four hundred years later, in 1912, a survey was made of the remaining Mennonites in the area, their names, with variant spellings, were almost solely those of the original Dutch settlers: Flemish names such as Klaassen, Dyck, Ens, Penner, and Regier; Frisian names such as Dirksen, Froese, Friesen, Janzen, and Martens. Only just a few names were of Polish origin, Sawatzky being perhaps the most common.

The forebears of those Mennonites who ultimately immigrated to Western Canada did not remain in the Vistula delta, but undertook a major trek elsewhere. In 1740, after they had lived for two centuries in the Polish lowlands, Frederick the Great began his long forty-six-year reign in nearby Prussia. It was during his rule of

militaristic expansion that various regions fell to his dominion, and in 1772 the Vistula delta did so. The Mennonites were guaranteed continued religious toleration by their new ruler but no longer military exemption.

At first the Mennonites escaped military service by payment of extra (and unfair) taxes, but it was immediately apparent that other impositions, such as decrees to stop further purchase of land by them, would severely affect the livelihood of the rapidly increasing population of Mennonites. At that time they numbered about twelve thousand souls. If their economic life was threatened, their religious and cultural identity would suffer too.

In 1786, Empress Catherine II of Russia issued, providentially it seems, an invitation to the Mennonites to settle on the uninhabited steppes of South Russia (or the Ukraine), north of the Black Sea. Certainly, the Mennonites looked upon the invitation as a godsend. That same fall two Mennonite representatives left the Vistula delta to examine the site and report back to their people. They were Jakob Hoeppner (my paternal great-great-great-great-grandfather) and Johann Bartsch. Their year-long round trip was not without its hazards, a presage of hardships to be endured in the next years by the emigrants. Hoeppner had broken his leg and Bartsch suffered from frozen toes.

One can imagine the feelings of these two men when they first found themselves fully out on the great Russian steppes, standing there, isolated, letting their eyes sweep across the rolling plains extending endlessly before them, even into the far reaches of Asia. Not a human habitation was in sight. The men were on the frontier of things where still occasionally bands of Nogaies, with Tatar blood in their veins, pursued their nomadic life as of old, galloping with swift horses through seas of grass, riding on and on—only, like inconsiderable specks, to disappear at last along the horizon. The two men, gazing, would seem lost in space, the silence of the land flowing over them with an almost audible pres-

Jakob Hoeppner monument at Mennonite Village Museum at Steinbach, Manitoba. The memorial was originally erected in the Chortitza colony in Russia and brought to Canada in 1973. Hoeppner (1748–1826) was one of the Mennonite deputies who inspected the Russian steppes before Mennonite settlement there from the Gdansk area, beginning in 1788. Hoeppner is the author's direct ancestor, back six generations.

Mennonite farmyard in Russia. After initial pioneer hardships, Mennonite farmers prospered on the Russian steppes.

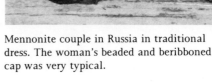

Mennonite couple in Russia in traditional dress. The woman's beaded and beribboned cap was very typical.

ence, a ringing stillness that throbbed in their ears. Alexander Borodin's orchestral tone-painting, *In the Steppes of Central Asia*, might well have provided the musical backdrop.

Here was country so different from Poland-Prussia—not reedy marshland but arid waste, a potentially fertile land but near desert in dry times with scourges of grasshoppers. It would be a sanctuary from what was happening in the Vistula delta in the last few years: of the Mennonites' total three-and-a-half century European existence, only some scant fifteen years had come under direct Prussian or German control, but the resulting conditions could not be tolerated. The two representatives would recommend removal to this new Promised Land. As it turned out, the land, with its vast plains, drought, and grasshoppers, would be a proving ground for another life in another homeland, in America, a century later. As with John the Baptist's sojourn in the desert, the Russian-steppe experience tested the Mennonites and strengthened their resolve.

All told, at least six thousand Mennonites, or half their population in the Vistula delta, left for settlement in Russia over the next years. There they would have exemption from military service but, as in Poland, there could be no proselytizing nor gaining of new members, including children, through intermarriage. The first group, 228 families along with those of Hoeppner and Bartsch, left in 1788, travelling partly by wagon train, partly by river barge. At their destination their first homes were sod shanties with walls halfway below ground level for greater security. Pilfering bands of thieves, it was discovered, roamed the countryside, and nothing was safe.

While the homes were intitially built on individual farms, as in Poland-Prussia, it was soon decided that small villages of some thirty families were much safer, and so began the Mennonite practice of living in small *Darpa*, which was carried over to North America. The houses clustered on two sides of a wide street, each with its flower plots in the front yard and orchards and vegetable gardens in back: the Mennonites, true to Dutch-

Display relating to silkworm culture at Mennonite Village Museum. Mennonites raised silkworms for silk production in Russia. The worms were fed leaves from the mulberry trees which were commonly grown about Mennonite homes.

men everywhere, loved tidy and beautiful home surroundings. Shade trees lined the street, which was also graced by a school and usually a church. Leading out from the village were narrow-strip farms and a common pasture, complete with youthful herdsman and his horn.

If the picture seems idyllic, it was to become so but only after generations of struggle—after the first decade there were doubts that the colony could survive. The first settlers built their villages at the junction of the mighty Dnieper River, which flows into the Black Sea, and its tributary, the Chortitza, now the environs of Zaporozh'ye. It was known as the Chortitza settlement, and when other colonies started, was referred to as the "Old Colony." By the turn of the century, 1800, it had some two thousand inhabitants.

In 1804 a second main colony was started to the southeast on the little Molochnaya River, which flows into the Sea of Azov. This was the Molochnaya settlement. To it 162 families came from Poland-Prussia initially, these in better financial straits than the Chortitza settlers had been, and the number of immigrants increased more than seven-fold by mid-century. By then many families were landless so that further daughter colonies were established as outgrowths of the original two settlements. The Bergthal colony, for example, grew out of Chortitza and had already been established by 1836.

The settlements were beginning to flourish and not only in size. A successful Molochnaya farmer, Johann Cornies, began to point the way in dryland farming methods, including summerfallowing, crop rotation, shelterbelts, and use of fertilizers—all of which would stand the Mennonites in good stead when they would immigrate to America later. In addition, they broadened their range of production. Not only were grains sown, but because of the climate there, watermelons turned out to be an excellent cash crop. A silk industry also thrived for a time, with many mulberry trees being planted to provide food for the silkworm.

It seemed that Mennonite hard work and efficiency, however, might eventually contribute to the group's undoing. As farms prospered and population steadily grew, the land-shortage bogey would once more haunt the Mennonites as it had on the Vistula after the Prussian take-over. By 1870 the Russian communities numbered forty-five thousand members, and in the original two colonies two-thirds of the families were without land. But it was a Russian proclamation that same year which brought things to a head and instigated another major trek.

In 1870 the government decided that no colonists in its empire should receive special privileges, that all should become good Russian citizens. This decision meant that the Russian language would be a subject of study in all schools, even private ones, and that military service would be compulsory. The Mennonites had ten years to accommodate themselves to this edict. But it was something they felt they could not live with, for their very culture seemed threatened. Could they maintain their ethnic identity if it should happen that their own language would be displaced? Appeals by them to the imperial city of St. Petersburg effected no change, and Mennonite leaders then turned elsewhere for a solution—to America.

Both Canada and the United States were looking for immigrants to populate their empty Western regions and make them fruitful. In Canada the first Dominion Lands Act was passed in 1872 and provided for free homestead land. Canada was particularly anxious to obtain settlers, knowing that its frontier had a more severe climate than its American counterpart. It was willing to offer the Mennonites military exemption in perpetuity, along with freedom of religion and language and control of schools. The Americans could not be as firm in their inducements.

In 1873 twelve Mennonite delegates left Russia to visit America and examine their prospective homes. They visited Manitoba, Minnesota, Dakota, Nebraska, and Kansas. On their return the Chortitza (Old Colony) and Bergthal representatives, as well as those from a strict separate congregation—*Kleine Gemeinde*, spoke for Canada. These groups tended to be more conservative (the *Kleine Gemeinde* had separated in 1812 from the *Grosse Gemeinde* in the Molochnaya colony), and despite harsher conditions on the Canadian prairie, their leaders felt they could achieve a safer, more isolated life there. The regular Molochnaya delegates represented a more liberal (and prosperous) community, and they recommended the United States as a future homeland. (The subsequent emigration followed these recommendations but not exclusively so: my maternal grandmother's people from Molochnaya did settle in Minnesota, but then so did my maternal grandfather's people—and they came from Chortitza.)

Whatever the destination, enthusiasm to emigrate was immediately at a fever pitch—so much so that the Russian government quickly realized that if something were not done it would be losing a host of excellent farmers, forty thousand all at once. It then offered a compromise proposal whereby Mennonites who chose to remain in Russia would engage in forestry labor instead of military service and in time of war would most likely substitute that with medical relief work. This appeased two-thirds of their number, particularly those who had the most to lose economically in any removal, and they opted to stay. The rest, about eighteen thousand souls, left Russia over the next years—eight thousand to Canada, the rest to the United States.

Among the immigrants were the landless, who sought a livelihood as a farming people; the steadfast, who would in no way compromise their principles regarding peace and service to the crown; the resistant to change, who feared any diminution of traditional values; and the adventurous, who wished "To strive, to seek, to find, and not to yield"[5] as their forebears had always done. With these various motivations the first group of Russian Mennonites arrived in Winnipeg on July 31, 1874.

House-barn at Heritage Village at Mountain Lake, Minnesota. This one, built at right angles, is similar to those originally built in the swamps of the Vistula delta in Poland when the Mennonites settled there from the Netherlands. Dredged-up earth from drainage canals became the farmyards, and there was little space for farm buildings.

They had come the last leg of their journey by steamboat down the Red River from Moorhead, Minnesota.

The immigrants settled on both sides of the Red River, where large tracts of land or reserves were set aside for them. The Bergthal contingent, who emigrated in three stages en masse from Russia, settled on the East Reserve of eight townships where Steinbach is now the principal business centre. The Old Colonists moved to the West Reserve, which consisted of seventeen townships and now includes the communities of Winkler, Morden, and Altona. This proved to be better land, and many Bergthalers moved there from the East Reserve in the next years. The *Kleine Gemeinde* settled in both areas, although only a few settled in the West Reserve—in the village of Rosenart on the Rat River. (Steinbach was at first a *Kleine Gemeinde* village.)

Once more the Mennonite people were back to basic pioneering struggles—building homes, breaking land, and establishing communities, all in a prairie wilderness. The first homes were sod huts dug into the ground, much like those their forebears had made when coming to Russia. Whereas in Russia the Mennonites had started the practice of grouping homes in villages as a protection against roving bandits, here the practice continued because it was now part of their tradition. With hard work, more than a hundred villages were established in the first ten years. As for breaking land, the labor seemed fruitless the first growing season (1875), for the entire crop was destroyed by grasshoppers. Next year frost struck. It was their religion, together with the pioneering spirit, which gave the Mennonites perseverance —that and no alternative!

In time the Mennonites' dryland farming practices overcame hardships. Yes, the Canadian prairies could support an agricultural population. Grain growing and dairying prospered; planted trees provided windbreaks across farms; sunflowers and domesticated native plum gave vivid color to farmyards. And windmills were built, the first one begun in 1877.

The sight again of a huge four-storey windmill towering into a cloud-filled sky, its sixty-foot sails slowly revolving with a gentle wind, must have answered some deep-felt need of a people who had fled their original home in the Netherlands so many years ago. Something there was that stirred in their racial memory, a realization that here on the prairies a vacuum was filled of which they had been only vaguely aware until they beheld the windmill's presence against the skyline. (An authentic replica, completed in 1972, is now the principal attraction at the Mennonite Village Museum at Steinbach.)

With increasing prosperity there came changes. Many villages broke up as farmers settled on individual homesteads and built up estates there. Some farmers looked beyond the borders of Manitoba—to the North-West Territories which would become the provinces of Saskatchewan and Alberta.

One group of settlers journeyed by locomotive in 1891

Windmill at Mennonite Village Museum. A working model built in 1972 under the direction of a Dutch millwright, it is an authentic replica of an earlier Steinbach windmill built in 1877 by A.S. Friesen, three years after the Mennonites first settled there.

to the neck of land between the North and South Saskatchewan Rivers, detrained there, and began the community of Rosthern, the centre of the main Mennonite settlement in Saskatchewan. (Among the original eleven families who homesteaded in the area were my grandparents. Their oldest son, almost seven at the time, was my father. Four miles east of the community, my other grandparents settled, coming from Minnesota later in the decade. Here a one-roomed rural school was built, named Bergthal after locations in Manitoba, and Russia, and here I took my elementary schooling.)

Later still, other settlements were established in various places in the West—at Swift Current and at Drake in Saskatchewan, at Didsbury in Alberta, and at Renata in British Columbia. (To this last location, on the Arrow

Lakes, my grandfather also journeyed in 1910 in order to look over the prospects, leaving his family behind at Rosthern. He stayed only a short while, but my father as a young bachelor worked there a year in the logging business. Today the centre is no more, but several Mennonite communities exist elsewhere in the province, at Abbotsford and Clearbrook, for example.)

Meanwhile, problems were occurring too. Although the first groups settling in Manitoba all represented the conservative wing of the Mennonites, the Bergthaler segment was more liberal in championing progress, in aligning itself more closely to Canadian practices in municipal affairs and in education. Its members ran for public office, and an enlightened number advocated the teaching of English in its parochial schools. To this end they opened a teacher-training school at Gretna in 1899.

The Old Colony members, on the other hand, were foremost in opposing any change, any innovation in their traditional lifestyle. Frictions arose within the Mennonite community and within the community at large and came to a head during World War I when a fervor of British patriotism swept the country. Provincial education authorities insisted on the attendance of all Mennonite children in public schools, where they would be assimilated into the Canadian way of life.[6] To the Old Colonists, and some to Bergthalers as well, this was another threat to their freedom—just as their people had experienced in Russia and in Poland-Prussia before that. And this when they thought they had been guaranteed control of their own language and schools on coming to Canada! (The promise of military exemption was kept, but this special status was also a source of friction. Note that later during World War II, while many Mennonites served in the armed forces, many others pleaded their cases as conscientious objectors and fulfilled nonmilitary roles.)

After the First World War when neither side, the government and the Old Colonists, would capitulate regarding the education question (and both could be as stub-

Modified house-barn, where a summer kitchen connects the two buildings, on a farm adjacent to author's boyhood home at Rosthern, Saskatchewan. The cross-patterned barn door was common in Mennonite barns in Russia.

born as the other and feel justified in being so), then these Mennonites looked elsewhere once more for a homeland. From 1922 to 1927 some eight thousand left Canada, six thousand for Mexico and nearly two thousand for Paraguay—and had to endure almost unbearable hardships there. In 1948 a second wave of two thousand (including my deskmate at Bergthal School near Rosthern) left for Paraguay. By then the chief concern was simply that modern living, with its movies and magazines and many conveniences, was luring young Mennonites from the simple ways of the past. Other concerns were expressed about the use of English in schools, as well as fears that the Mennonites' exemption from military service would not be granted in future years. In each instance the ones who remained were those who could adapt to changing times and become part of the larger Canadian society, could become an important part of its rich mosaic.

The loss of some Old Colonists to Mexico and Paraguay did not decrease the number of Mennonites in Western Canada. Another exodus was taking place, this time into Canada and again from Russia. About two-and-a-half times as many Mennonites immigrated here in the 1920s as were leaving for Latin America. The first trainload of newcomers, six hundred of them, arrived at Rosthern in 1923 (my parents were there to watch the arrival), and their fellow emigrees were soon crowding stations in other centres. And at the time when another two thousand Mennonites left for Paraguay in the late 1940s, the ending of World War II created a similar-sized influx to Canada of more Russian Mennonites. Although Western Canadian Mennonites can all say that Russia was their immediate former homeland, the ones already here were becoming Canadianized. The newcomers, however, needed a label to distinguish them, and so among the Mennonites they were called "Russlanders" (*Russlenda*).

The Russlanders were to play a significant role in Mennonite affairs over the succeeding years, and it is well to take a better look at their background. They stemmed from the people who had stayed behind when their fellow Mennonites had gone to America a half century earlier. They had stayed because they tended to be of that number who were *not* landless but already had flourishing farms. Somehow, having a productive land base and security in closely knit villages, they would get along with new Russian edicts affecting language and education.

It could be stated that the Russlanders were less principled than their emigrating brethren of the 1870s in accommodating themselves to serving the crown, even in forestry units, where such service might still contribute to militarism indirectly; that they were more materialistic in allowing economic considerations to influence their decision to remain in Russia. On the other hand, they could be thought of as more progressive in their thinking, more willing to adapt to changing circumstances and make the best of it. In any case these people did come to have, in the additional years spent in Russia, a somewhat different outlook, a different mind-set, from those Mennonites who had departed for America earlier.

The forestry service gave the young men a chance to mix with their fellow Russians, and this experience could not have been other than broadening for them. Their own schools meanwhile were improving. Mennonites had always stressed a basic education for all their members—indeed, they made attendance compulsory in their parochial schools as early as 1843—decades ahead of its being so introduced in schools in Great Britain, for example.[7] But those early Mennonite schools stressed only a practical literacy and arithmetic (and Bible study). Now with the Russlanders, however, their school system had come to provide for a continuation of studies so that some men even went on to university, almost two hundred in 1914, and entered the professions, including engineering and medicine. In this regard the Russlanders were ahead of their counterparts in Canada, where if a select few obtained post-secondary education, it was usually a short training to enable them to teach in a rural school or nurse in a local hospital.

The Russlanders of course were not undergoing pioneer hardships and privations. Their farms were prosper-ing, and now their industries underwent much expansion. When the Mennonites first came to Russia, they were a self-sufficient farming people. Most farmers also practised some trade to supply the needs of the village (thus my mother's one grandfather was a tailor as well as a farmer; her other grandfather was a shoemaker). But with the success of grain growing on the steppes, combined with greater expertise through better education, the Russlanders built huge factories to produce farm machinery (and not just for themselves) and large mills to grind feed and flour. These two industries were a natural outgrowth of their traditional way of life, especially the milling business. The Mennonites had used windmills for centuries, but here in Russia, instead of their use in controlling water levels, the mills could be used solely for grinding grain, and the entrepreneurs built steam mills, which were more reliable.

Although milling was the largest industry, there were many others—more than five hundred in total.[8] There was also some activity in the humanities, in writing local histories (and printing them) and in painting, but this was far exceeded by humanitarian efforts, something which has become ingrained in Mennonite culture. Hospitals were built, as were orphanages, nursing homes, and even a centre for the mentally ill.

All of this was possible because the basic employment of farming, through steady application, was so successful. Farms were becoming grand holdings, and farm homes—stately residences. It was a point of pride to boast how many steam mills were located on one's property. (A comparison can again be made with what life was like among the Mennonites in Canada then, particularly among those who were forging farmsteads west of Manitoba: when the first Russlanders arrived in Rosthern, my parents were living in an uninsulated fourteen by twenty-foot shack.)

It is easy, where there is worldly success, for individuals to see themselves singled out by Providence—and a short step from that to identify any of their successful enterprises as religiously virtuous. The Russlanders' own thriving economy could well translate the natural Mennonite piety into a purposeful pious attitude among some of the most successful, and this attitude could be manifested in a looking down upon the impoverished Russian peasants who lived nearby and were hired to work on the large estates. This attitude, where evident, could not have but been sensed by those to whom it was directed.

And then came World War I, the Russian Revolution of 1917, and the civil war and anarchic state which followed. The military exemption which the Mennonites enjoyed during the Great War made them already the target of a hate campaign, and the later communist takeover would in time dissolve their handsome estates. But it was the civil strife and anarchy which wrought the most immediate havoc. Livestock was confiscated; people were killed. (Two of my father's relatives were disposed of: one was led away from his home at night and never heard of again; the other was taken to a hill overlooking his village, where a windmill stood, and shot there.)

Roving hordes of ruthless ne'er-do-wells plundered the villages in an absolute reign of terror which lasted three years. Not only were men murdered, but women were raped, homes burned—and then on to the next village. In one instance eighty-one of eighty-three men in one Mennonite village were killed in a single night. As if such incidents were not bad enough, epidemics of disease were spread by the perpetrators, leaving people dead by the thousands. The Chortitza settlement or Old Colony seemed to have been hit the hardest, both by crime and by disease. Some one thousand to fifteen hundred people there died of typhus. Then in 1921–22 drought and famine struck everyone, with people lying dead along the roadsides.[9]

So about twenty-one thousand Russlanders, fleeing with little but personal belongings, came to Canada in the 1920s, largely through the efforts of the Reverend David Toews of Rosthern, who was president of the newly organized Mennonite Board of Colonization. Another Rosthern resident, Gerhard Ens, who held the dual post of Dominion Government immigration officer and Canadian Pacific Railway colonization agent, also helped to facilitate the project. Financial aid came from Mennonites across America and from the Netherlands as well. Some of the Russlanders at least had high expectations of their new homeland and, although thankful for any refuge after the turmoil and heartbreak they had been through, must have been disappointed too. They had left well established farming estates and businesses (as they were before the war) and arrived among a host people who were just coming out of the Canadian West's pioneer era. Whereas they on the whole had been big operators, aggressive in pursuing materials goals, their Canadian counterparts might better be described—and this again is a generalization—as akin to the unassuming yeomen of Thomas Gray's famous elegy, content with their "sequester'd vale of life."[10]

The arrival of the Russlanders had several effects on the Mennonite populace. Many of the newcomers were better educated, with high school education, some with college training. It was natural for them, once they had served a year's labor on a farm, as required by immigration regulations, to assume leadership roles in the community as teachers and ministers. New churches were built—for Russlanders were forward in pursuing spiritual goals too—and schools as well. One writer has spoken of an intellectual awakening occurring in Mennonite districts.[11] Private secondary schools were revived, with the teachers stamping them with their particular mind-set; graduating students went on to a variety of professions.

The ambitious nature of the Russlanders thrust them into the forefront of things so that among the non-Mennonite community there was a tendency to take them as representative of all Mennonites in Western Canada even though they were a minority. As the more educated, they were becoming spokesmen for the entire group. Where there was any antipathy felt by outsiders to an ethnic group, it seemed for a while to gain impetus from the very forwardness of the Russlanders among the Mennonites, however it revealed itself—in shrewd business ways, in evangelical endeavor, or in retention of their language (despite the fact that they quickly learned the English of their new land). And for similar reason there was some antipathy between the two groups of Mennonites themselves. (One is reminded here of the friction between the Frisian and the Flemish wings of the Mennonite people which existed during their Vistula delta sojourn and carried over into Russia.) In time such feelings rightfully dissipated.

Today the Mennonites of Western Canada are well respected in whatever communities they live. For they have widely dispersed, with well over one-hundred thousand living in the four provinces. No longer mainly a farming people (many of the original Dutch forebears were artisans), most now live in cities, and centres like Winnipeg, Vancouver, and Saskatoon have significant Mennonite populations. The largest number, some sixty thousand, still live in the province of Manitoba, where Mennonites first settled when they fled Europe. Half of that number live in Winnipeg, the capital.

It has been a long and winding road that the people of Dutch origin have travelled since they began to leave their native Netherlands in 1530, surviving persecution and hardship, persevering always with the strength of their religious faith, the love that would not let them go—on to Poland, to Russia, to Canada (and midwestern United States). Winnipeg now has the largest concentration of Mennonites of any city in the world and in Mennonite history.

Someone has said that if you would bring four Mennonite men together, you would probably have the makings of a good male quartet for singing, and the observation is not far from the truth. Music is important to these people, and their choirs have achieved international attention. For a people who through much of their history led lives focused within their own group, it is chiefly in the present century that such contributions to society at large have been recognized. And there will be more contributions to follow in the years ahead—in painting, writing, politics, science—for Mennonites are now engaged in every kind of labor and profession.

Perhaps most widely known of Mennonite activities is the relief work, social assistance, and agricultural development carried on through the Mennonite Central Committee (MCC) in Third World countries or anywhere else where there is need. Young volunteers, some one thousand strong in fifty countries, devote two or three years of their lives to serving their fellowman. It was this kind of fellow feeling within their own religious group which helped them overcome adversity in the past. With secure lives at last in their Canadian or American homeland, they can fulfill a basic tenet of Menno Simons's teaching so long ago—to translate their faith into deeds—and extend it worldwide.

TWO

A Distinct Language

When the forebears of Western Canadian Mennonites fled the Netherlands following 1530, they naturally spoke the Dutch language. Their church services were in Dutch, for early church literature was printed in that language, and their written communications were in Dutch. However, what is not commonly known, even among present-day young Mennonites, is that these forebears continued to use the Dutch language in their sermons and literature for the next 250 years, more or less for their entire sojourn in the Vistula delta region.

Of course this region is in the Gdansk area of modern Poland, and it was Polish aristocrats who first offered the Mennonites refuge there. It would not be likely that the closely knit Mennonites would opt for a Slavic tongue. But the area was a borderline one between the Poles and the Germans, with the latter people enlarging their dominion ever eastward until finally what had been happening demographically was made so politically: the first partitioning of Poland occurred in 1772 when the delta became Prussian territory. Thus the Mennonites had German or Prussian neighbors too, but as with the Poles, the Mennonites lived aloof from them and steadfastly maintained Dutch as their official language almost to the time of their removal to Russia.

Sometime well before the Mennonites left the Vistula delta, they did adopt West Prussian Platt or *Plautdietsch* as their everyday language. Exactly when in the seventeenth century this occurred cannot be determined now because its adoption would have been a gradual process, words and phrases mixing with their native Dutch, which was not that different a language. The speech was used in conducting day-to-day business with one's Mennonite associates and in conversing with family members at home. Finally when the Mennonites were settled in Russia at the close of the eighteenth century, *Plautdietsch* became the real, serviceable language of their culture, the ethnic glue giving the people their distinct identity.

Since there are some misconceptions about the *Plautdietsch* language in the public mind, it is well to clear up the matter now.[1] The term *Plautdietsch* when translated means "Low German" (*Plaut* is "low": cognate word— "flat"); and Mennonites speak of it as Low German. (This English name already creates some confusion, for it is more generally used to signify a family of languages, as explained in the next paragraphs.) Somehow the conception arose that the language, because it bore the qualification "Low," was therefore a lower or crude form of standard German or a dialect derived from it. This is simply not so.

Plautdietsch is *not* a dialect of present-day literary German; it is, in the form spoken by the Mennonites, a distinct speech of its own. The "Low" of Low German is a geographical reference to the *low*lands of northern Europe—the Netherlands and northern Germany along the Baltic coast. Sometime after 500 A.D. and continuing until the eighth century, there transpired what is called the Second Consonantal or High German Sound Shift, described by Grimm's Law, in the West Germanic languages of Europe. This phenomenon differentiated the Low German languages (so-called because they were centered in the coastal lowlands) from the High German languages (which were centered south of the higher Harz region of Germany). Thus modern German, a High German language, separated and took an independent course from the Low German languages more than a millenium ago.

The Low German languages include not only *Plautdietsch* (and its direct ancestor Old Saxon) but other lowland speech—Dutch, Flemish, Frisian, and English (there has been a tendency in recent years for authorities to consider Frisian and English as a distinct branch of West Germanic). It is little wonder that the Mennonites of the Vistula delta readily adopted *Plautdietsch* as their everyday language when it had such close kinship to the Dutch they had always spoken. Canadian writer Paul Hiebert in his book, *Doubting Castle*, 1976, speaks of the language's Dutch base,[2] but it would be more precise to say that the two languages have the same base.

The question of readily adopting (High) German as a church language by the Mennonites was altogether another matter, however. Some form of Low German had been the language of the area in the distant past, and had been used in the late Middle Ages, for instance, by the merchants of the Hanseatic League in conducting their Baltic trade. Some form too had served as a literary language even longer, but with the decline of the League, the language gradually gave way to standard German as the predominant language. Now in the eighteenth century, German was the business language of the Mennonites' Prussian neighbors. Then there was as well, as a greater inducement for change, the eloquent Luther translation of the Bible.

So it was that in 1762 a sermon in German was given for the first time in a Danzig Mennonite church—but there was such an uproar among the members that this experiment was not tried again for another five years. Dutch had been the language of the pulpit for more than two centuries, it was the language of their fathers and their fathers before them, and the members were not going to change things. But change is inevitable when times are ripe for it, and six years after the momentous sermon, the Dutch hymnbook was replaced by one in German.

Hans van Steen, a prominent Mennonite minister in Danzig at the time, bewailed the change in language. Till his death in 1781, just seven years before the trek to Russia began, he continued to preach in Dutch and keep the church records in that language. His successor did not do so, but more than one member in leaving for Russia still packed a Dutch Bible[3] among his belongings as well as the Dutch *Martyrs Mirror*. A German edition of this last book did not appear until after the first wave of settlers had left the Vistula delta. In Russia these settlers still thought of themselves as Dutch.[4]

A parallel can be drawn at this point with the situation regarding the Old Colony Mennonites in Canada in the first decades of the twentieth century. They did not want to change language either. Only now the choice was German, the language whose introduction in Mennonite churches in the eighteenth century had caused such displeasure. The Old Colonists wished to retain it in their own Canadian elementary schools in preference over English, while the government of the day thought English was needed in order to Canadianize its citizens.

The Old Colonists' stand represents one of the most ironic occurrences in Mennonite history. English, after all, with its affiliation with Low German languages and with the Mennonites' native Dutch and ethnic *Plautdietsch*, should in that sense have been as akin to them as German.[5] German, it seems, had come to mean more to Mennonites during their sojourn in Russia than it had in Poland-Prussia. But there was another factor at play. German also spelled a certain exclusiveness to them— they were not going to let go easily their right to be uniquely themselves.

One can appreciate these people's position in resisting the learning of English. *Plautdietsch* was already learned in the home, and familiarity with German was gained at church while its proper use was taught at school. The government's assimilation program was then not a case of Mennonite children studying English as a second language but as a *third* language.[6] (I too learned *Plautdietsch* as my first language but was not introduced to German speech at all until some years later, and I can still recall looking askance at the speaker and wondering what foreign tongue she was speaking.)

The Old Colony Mennonites' insistence upon their use of German in Canada stemmed also from what had occurred in Russia during these Mennonites' one-century stay there. Although *Plautdietsch* remained the real language of the people—the *Folkjsproak* (folk speech), it was not a means of written communication, for its grammar and spelling were not formalized—the Mennonites had no standardized system for writing it down (this book uses such a recently devised system). German, which supplanted Dutch as the language of the church, could fill this role nicely. Thus German became not only the "Sunday language" of sermons and hymn singing but the language of business correspondence, of any written epistles for that matter, and of speech with non-Mennonites, it being a world-wide language. The names of Mennonite villages, since they were written down, were also in German (that is, those that were not in Russian).

One is reminded here of Julius K. Toews's delightfully titled essay, "We Spoke English to the Horses and Low German to the Cows" (in *Manitoba Mennonite Memories*, 1974),[7] describing his pioneer boyhood in Canada. A related dichotomy must have existed in Russia where *Plautdietsch* was the language in which the Mennonites worked, played, and did all their thinking. It was the vehicle of their rich folklore—nursery rhymes, games, and maxims—which is the subject of this book. German, on the other hand, was the language for formal occasions, including religious services.

The German language has a euphonious quality to it, a melodic flow of line (arising in part, I think, from its varied adjectival declensions), something which writers in English must consciously strive for but which occurs naturally in German. Mennonites in Russia, once having become accustomed to reading and hearing passages from the German Bible since their childhood, would not wish to let go this part of their heritage when they moved to Canada. They are like people today who are used to hearing the King James Version of the Bible and

Hoeppner's Bible at Mennonite Village Museum. It dates from 1643.

care to have no other (granted the poetic nature of this translation).

To the Mennonites it eventually seemed that the German Bible was at the heart of their religion, and since Bible study was included in their own school curriculum, German seemed to be integral with their education as well. Altogether, German was the language they "wore" when meeting non-Mennonites, the language in which other people saw them, the language by which they kept themselves apart from these people, the language which they themselves felt gave them respectability. But at home they spoke *Plautdietsch*! And doing so may have answered some deep-felt unconscious need: among common modern languages homely *Plautdietsch* most resembles Dutch, their ancestral tongue.

When the Mennonites first settled in Canada, the same use of the two languages obtained—only now Julius Toews and his fellows were speaking a third language, English, to the horses (which had been bought from Anglo-Saxon neighbors and understood commands only in this language). To the Anglo-Saxon neighbors, these new immigrants of Dutch national origin seemed solely German. After all, the Mennonites spoke German to government officials, used it in their written correspondence and local newspapers and in their church services, and even gave their villages these quaint German names—"Rosenhof" (yard of roses), "Schoenfeld" (beautiful field), and "Blumenort" (place of flowers). All this was as it had been in Russia.

Then, too, the neighbors already knew about the Mennonites who had settled earlier in Ontario and had, in fact, provided financial aid for the new settlers, and *they* were of German stock. The neighbors did not realize that the two groups of Mennonites, although of the same religion, were different peoples, with different surnames and different customs (for example, the foods they ate). The Mennonites of Western Canada, from their treks across Europe, had developed a rich and varied culture unique to them. The German they spoke on formal occasions was a language borrowed along the way and made their own: as a people they knew little of Germany's history, for they had never really been part of it.[8] Their adopted *Plautdietsch* had been with them a longer time and was the language of their culture. It was not a bastardized German. (It is no wonder, then, that the *Encyclopedia Americana*, 1983, refers to these Mennonites always as being of *Dutch* ancestry.[9])

So affairs remained in the new land until the Russlanders came. They had stayed in Russia a half century longer and had undergone some cultural changes in the interval. The one that concerns us here has to do with language. Reference has previously been made to the czarist government's avowed attempts to Russianize its country's citizens during this time. This fact, we know, prompted the Mennonites' original emigration from Russia beginning in 1874. The Mennonites who remained, that is, the Russlanders, found that they could best maintain some unique identity by emphasizing their cultural connections with their former homeland in the Vistula delta, and this was now part of Prussia or Germany.

These Mennonites, as has been already stated, were collectively more successful operators in farming or business, more progressive than their fellows who had left for America at the first sign of Russianization. Perhaps it was opportunistic for the Russlanders at this time to look to Germany now that it was becoming a world power under Otto von Bismarck, first chancellor of the modern German empire. Perhaps, as well, it was plainly nostalgic to look back to other times—like the farmers in Gabrielle Roy's short story, "Hoodoo Valley," who found that "each new evil chases out the last; having forgotten the persecutions that had forced them to leave [their former homeland], their hearts retained nothing of it but the most tender recollections."[10] In any case, although it was now a century since the Mennonites had left Poland-Prussia, there was developing among some of the Russlanders a conscious effort to Germanize themselves, to speak more German, and to look disdainfully at *Plautdietsch*.[11]

This attitude was carried over to Canada when the Russlanders emigrated there after the Russian Revolution. Many of them were well-educated, as has been said earlier, and became teachers in schools in Mennonite settlements. Leaders in the community themselves, they were training future leaders: their influence was extensive. The emphasis that some of them gave to the German language was good—the study of any language is worthwhile—and German, unlike *Plautdietsch*, was a standardized language, widely written as well as spoken. But such emphasis was often accompanied by a downgrading of the *Plautdietsch*.

In some families so influenced by this attitude—or in those families, not necessarily Russlander, who already had a propensity to think in similar vein—it became almost a point of snobbery for the parents to say that their children spoke only High German at home; that is, they did *not* speak *Plautdietsch*.[12] Then, too, one had the other extreme, where some Mennonite parents, wishing to be fully "Canadian," boasted that their children could speak only English. In either case, *Plautdietsch* received short shrift.

In some instances Mennonite children were forbidden by teachers to speak their ethnic language on the school playground. Again, *Plautdietsch* was considered an inferior language. Admittedly, this admonition had its practical rationale, for beginning students, speaking only *Plautdietsch*, would thus have to learn English more quickly. (When I began my teaching career in a one-roomed rural school, I was instructed by my superintendent to follow this procedure with my Mennonite beginners—the year was 1952!)

All of these concerns, seemingly so important at the time, were just a passing phase in the history of the Mennonites of Western Canada. Although *Plautdietsch*, as spoken by our Mennonites, has all but vanished in Europe where it originated—only about one hundred people living in the Gdansk area of Poland still speak it—it does live on in America, particularly in the breakaway Mennonite colonies in Mexico and Paraguay. In Canada its role, versus the German language, has in fact undergone a reversal of sorts. German now is little used in Mennonite church services as congregation members prefer English. Many younger members can no longer read or write the language. It is beginning to be reserved for chaplains in Mennonite nursing homes, where the elderly people, understandably, wish to hear the word of God in the language of Luther's Bible.

Plautdietsch, on the other hand, is undergoing what might be called a kind of revival. It is probably true that in the long term the language will slowly fade away. Perhaps the present generation realizes that if this colorful, down-to-earth speech is to endure at all, then its wealth of substance, in song and story, must be published now—hence this collection of folklore. But there has already been much literature written and preserved, even going back several decades, pointing the way for present-day authors in *Plautdietsch*.

In naming a few selected writers of these special works, one cannot help omitting other accomplished ones, but the following should be mentioned: Arnold Dyck for his famous, and humorous "Koop enn Bua opp Reise" series of stories, begun in the 1930s and now newly collected in one volume by editor Al Reimer; Fritz Senn (Gerhard Friesen) for his simple, moving poetry of everyday Mennonite life; Reuben Epp for his beautiful recordings of spoken *Plautdietsch* literature; and Jack Thiessen and also Herman Rempel for their resolute work on Mennonite Low German dictionaries. Mention as well could be made of Margaret Epp, whose first novel in the mid-1960s, although in English, had all its conversational dialogue in *Plautdietsch* speech patterns, and of Veleda (Unger) Goulden, who compiled and illustrated a coloring-book collection of Low German nursery rhymes. Also noteworthy are *Harvest: Anthol-*

ogy of Mennonite Writing in Canada, 1874–1974, ed. George K. Epp and others, 1974, which has a section of *Plautdietsch* writing, and *A Sackful of Plautdietsch*, ed. Al Reimer, Anne Reimer, and Jack Thiessen, 1983, which is a collection devoted solely to this writing.[13]

With such evidence of renewed interest in *Plautdietsch* literature, it may be that there will be much more forthcoming presently and that *Plautdietsch* as a language will yet live on in the foreseeable future and continue to add to Canada's rich cultural mosaic.

THREE

A Rich Folklore

The *Plautdietsch* of the Mennonites of Western Canada is a language "of the people, by the people, for the people."[1] It is a down-to-earth language quite capable of being a vehicle of a people's folklore, giving us insights into their way of life as revealed in nursery rhymes and games, songs and riddles, and many maxims pertaining to every aspect of that life.

Such a homely language is needed by a people who through most of their history have been a farming people, enduring the vicissitudes of time and weather in raising their crops and feeding their families. What really tested their endurance, though, were the harsh alternations in political climate as they trekked from country to country for a chance to live their peaceful lives. For they were *The People, Yes*—like the protagonists in Carl Sandburg's famous work, able to persevere with the "nourishing earth for rootholds."[2] Their treks went from their native Netherlands to Poland-Prussia, to Russia, and eventually to America. All regions played a part in the development of their folklore.

Mennonite *Plautdietsch* is also a colorful, sensuous language. Many of the words have in their pronunciation an appeal to one's kinesthetic sense. The mere saying of them seems to imitate and re-inforce what is being said: one seems to feel the "meaning" with one's lips and the muscles of the throat and vocal cords. Thus the verb *schlucke* (to swallow) has not only the vowel sound appropriate to the action named but the final syllable tends to give the sensation of the Adam's apple bobbing back down in the final act of swallowing. The English word "gulp" has these features too, but such examples are more common in *Plautdietsch*. Folklore in this language cannot help but be vivid.

Using this vivid language, the Mennonite men and women—whether in Poland or Russia—composed their rhymes and maxims as accompaniments to some everyday experiences or as afterthoughts to some events (and hence forethoughts to others yet to come). The items for the most part were probably composed by a single individual, but a song such as "The *Brummels* Song" seems more likely to have had communal authorship. In either case, the oral transmission from generation to generation and from region to region must have altered some of the words and/or added others. Some early items stemming from the Netherlands, and in Dutch, would have been translated into *Plautdietsch*. The same would have been true with selected German and Russian items later on in Mennonite history. And they all found their way to America, where still further changes, however minor by then, could take place.

This collection, in *Plautdietsch* and English translation, starts with the nursery rhymes, the first bit of folklore a Mennonite child would hear and remember. From this large quantity is chosen, for the chapter entitled "Rhymes of the Homelands," a half dozen which have a direct reference to the four regions in which Mennonite people have lived. Note that there are at least two rhymes which definitely have a Dutch origin (Nos. 6-2 and 10-2), for their counterparts have been found in collections of Dutch folk rhymes.[3] However, neither of them depicts a scene which is uniquely Dutch.

Whether or not the rhyme chosen to represent the Netherlands is in fact from that country is not clear, but it does speak of a windmill, which is emblematic of the Netherlands—and also of Western Canadian Mennonites. Their Dutch forebears built them in their native land, then used them in Poland to drain the Vistula marshes, continued their use as flour mills in Russia, and finally built them again on first immigrating to Manitoba. The description in the rhyme is a homely one in which warm family relationships are important. Presumably a mother is calling her son to dinner. All seems to be right with the world: goslings are at home in their natural habitat, possibly a drainage canal, while there is enough wind to drive the mill of "Father," the breadwinner.

The next rhyme specifically mentions Poland, where the Mennonites moved while seeking refuge from religious persecution in the Netherlands. The rhyme could refer to that journey or, more likely, to a family conversation after the next major trek—to Russia—with the girl reflecting on her chance for marriage in her former homeland. The opening line, "*Kromm, eromm,*" may simply be nonsense words, characteristic of nursery

rhymes, but it might also indicate that the girl in question is no family beauty ("*kromm*" means crooked). Whatever the case she has some spunk and will go farther afield if necessary to get a bridegroom.

There are three rhymes dealing with Russia. One refers to *kopecks*, small Russian coins, and affairs in this verse seem to be running smoothly. But the rhyme in which Marie has her orchard fruit seized by a Russian hired man seems to presage the eventual communist takeover following the Revolution. The third rhyme depicts, in contradistinction to the windmill rhyme, a world gone wrong, with children crying, calves bleating, and Russians faring forth, apparently in control. How will it all end?

The ending, a happy one, came with immigration to America, and the representative rhyme here is really an amalgam of some seasonal observations. The first two lines depict a common springtime event—an extra large wash hanging on the fence to dry, for this was a time when the indoors must be renewed in appearance just as was the greening world outdoors. The final two lines come from my grandmother, my mother's mother. The "*Jung-febiela*" was her name for our meadowlark, which in its blithe song, was either reminding farmers to be a-stirring—seeding-time would soon be upon them—or that there was no very great haste—each time it sang there were always yet another five days to go. The ambivalence is typical of folklore, where an individual can read a variety of meanings into the literature.

All the other "Nursery Rhymes" comprise the next section of the collection. While previous rhymes were considered in some detail—they gave insights into the various Mennonite homelands—it is not the purpose of this book to do so with each item in a section. Some general comments, however, may prove helpful to the reader.

More than a dozen of the rhymes are about foods and eating—something of great importance to small children. To the very small, milk is the sought-after food, and there is a rhyme about a child drinking his little belly full before falling asleep. Cookies are a special treat for older children, and the rhyme about "New Year's Cookies" (the traditional holiday fritters called *Portseltje*) is one of the most familiar to Mennonites. In it there is a heart-warming picture of a boy seeing a chimney smoking and then running to the house because he believes the housewife inside must be making these cookies. If he were given as much as five of them, his gratitude would know no bounds—he would wish the cook all of heaven's realm.

There are several related rhymes. One is of another boy who finds no one at home to welcome him except a mouse and so cannot ask even for bread and butter; one gives a simple recipe of another kind of cookie. Children seem to be always hungry, and there are rhymes as well about that fact and the dire consequences of eating too much (or of being too finicky in eating).

In English folklore there is the story about an old woman not being able to get home tonight because her pig will not jump over a stile, dog will not chase pig, stick will not beat dog, fire will not burn stick, and so on, until a chain of events can be actuated. This kind of line patter is also found in a *Plautdietsch* rhyme, beginning "*Mejchel, prejchel,*" where the end result of a progression—from bird, to hay, to cow, to milk, to cream, to butter, to weaver—is a pair of new shoes. Shoes are important to children, almost as much as food, so that more than one rhyme deals with them. The most endearing one speaks for children's compassion in sympathizing with little goslings (and how often do goslings crop up in the rhymes!). In this verse the shoester has lost his little wooden gosling last or foot form so that the little animals must go barefoot in the cold weather. The details of shoemaking would be well known to Mennonite children because in the olden days their shoes were often homemade.

Another subject of interest to small children is going somewhere. Three of the nursery rhymes here have words—nonsense words, if need be—rhymed with children's names: *Jeat* (George)—*schmeat, Aunn* (Ann)—*aun,* '*Trien* (Katherine)—*Lien, Mitsch* (Mary)—*pitsch, Soa* (Sarah)—*foa,* and *Johaun* (John)—*aun.* A child so lucky as to have one of these very names would feel directly involved, and honored, when hearing the rhyme recited.[4] Horses are the means of locomotion in the first two nursery rhymes, but the third has cats and mice in harness, something quite possible in a child's imaginative world.

The world becomes pure fantasy where one animal hitches up another, as we find in "Lambkin's Little Mare." This is a playtime realm, where all is song and dance, that we find in other rhymes too—billy goats prancing, goslings running away, and children playing fiddles and flutes. Alas, another musical instrument, the *Brommtopp* (New Year's drum), although adding to the holiday atmosphere with its sonorous *brumming,* takes the children back to the real world of study and hard work. All the New Year's cookies, apparently, have been eaten.

"Nursery Games," the next section in the book, are rhymes too, but they all involve actions. The baby is lovingly played with and educated in its world—a world of fingers and toes, cheeks and noses—long before there is any conscious awareness. The games are of three main groups, the first one involving teasing play between mother, or older member of the family, and the baby. The mother recites an appropriate verse and then may bump heads with the baby, pull its hair, shake its foot, or pretend to punch it, all in affectionate good fun.

Of equal fun to little children are those nursery games where the rhymes have an up-and-down rhythm as in a cradle or on a rocking horse. There are several in *Plautdietsch,* and notice the onomatopoeic sounds of these lines, all from different rhymes and all with nonsense words: "*Schockel, Schockel, scheia; Troch, Troch, treitje; Hupps, hupps, hupps, hupps, seedatje;* and *Hutt-re-putt, hutt-re-putt, hutt-re-putt.*" Like "Rockabye, Baby," one of the rhymes has the baby fall, not from a bough that breaks, but from a load of hay. The child experiencing this "fall" in the game eagerly anticipates the "surprise" and begs to be surprised again and again. (Surprises crop up in other ways: in one rhyme a tomcat lays not an egg—unusual enough in itself—but a rooster!) The rocking-horse nursery rhymes are also fascinating because of the destinations ridden to, Grandma's house and a mill—or because of the varying types of steed described in "Hoot-re-poot."

As in English rhymes again, there are *Plautdietsch* counting games. But instead of toes being counted and piggies going to market, we have fingers shaking down plums from a tree and then gathering them up. In still other rhymes, fingers might be paired as man and wife, described as butter lickers and louse squishers, or gestured in mock preparation of food. All actions teach the child to count.

In one rhyme where fingers and hands are used with other gestures to dramatize a more complex event, we are reminded of the familiar "Pat-a-cake." Another rhyme, describing the baking of biscuits, has the accompanying music of an old German hymn.[5] The lyrics have special attraction, for it is the children who are the little biscuits which Mother has made.

"Children's Games" are for older children. Where someone must be "it"—for instance, in a game of tag—then there needs to be a rhyme to select the individual. This collection has three, all of which are filled with nonsense words, much as "Ickle, Bickle, Black Buckle" is. Separate rhymes can be chanted at the person being "it," once the tag game has started.

More involved games are those involving questions and answers or circle formations. One set of questions and answers is merely the preliminary to a kind of "Blindman's Buff," only here the blindfolded person is called "blind cow." In another game, what amounts to a kind of "Pum-pum-pull-away," a set dialogue takes place between a "Mother Goose" and her "little ones" (those goslings again!) who stand some distance away. When she calls them, a "wolf" (always the villain) tries to tag them. Implicit in the game is the idea of safety and comfort of mother and home.

Two further games are very much like their English counterparts, "Ring-a-round-a-rosie" and "London Bridge Is Falling Down." The *Plautdietsch* version of this last one also has an accompanying melody. There is indeed a sameness to children's games the world over.

In *Plautdietsch* folklore there are several "Songs" which depict a world in which anything goes or anything is possible. They are sung just for the hilarity of it, although one is for a specific occasion. The songs belie the public notion that the lives of earlier-day Mennonites were focused only on serious, staid matters. Five songs are included in this collection, and three of them have just a verse or two. In one the singers are going to creep into a farmer's cellar and drink his wine; in another they are celebrating a couple's dying because then they will inherit some buttered bread and a chicken foot.

The most hilarious of the songs is "The *Brummels* Song"—if one can stand hearing all nineteen verses. They proceed, through question and answer, in telling the tale of a man who boils his shirt (in washing it), and finding a louse in it, does not let this discovery go to waste. The last verse proclaims the man is daft, something the listener already suspected long ago.

"The *Brommtopp* Song" also has many verses, some dozen of them, but these are only fantastic in the wishes they convey. This is the New Year's song that mummers sing as they go from house to house to wish the inhabitants in turn the best of fortune: the master a golden table with dishes of fried fish and wine, the wife a golden crown and a well-behaved son, down to the swineherd a cudgel to chase his pigs. All this is to the accompaniment of the famous *Brommtopp*, with the mummers' hope that they may receive some coins or at least some New Year's cookies for their efforts.[6]

"Riddles, Jokes, and Tongue-Twisters" are further examples of Mennonite good fun. The three riddles here are fairly involved in that a rhyme of from four to eight lines is presented which describes an object or objects. No direct question is asked, but the listener must guess from the activity in the rhyme just what is being referred to. Modern-day children would have a little trouble guessing, for instance, that a "jingle-man" represents a team of horses in jingling harness.

Plautdietsch humor tends to be rather droll. This is seen in one of the jokes where a man tells what he had for dinner—"Nothing I said *no* to, and everything I could say *yes* to." In the *Plautdietsch* version the drollery is more apparent because the appeal is typically more to the senses: the abstract terms, "yes" and "no," become concrete, for they are spoken of as coverings over the food.

There is a kind of waggish humor too in the tongue-twisters—in making light of such unlikely activities as women washing diapers or one man willingly carrying a second man piggyback through a dovecote thick with dove droppings. It is not the barnyard association which provides the humor in this second example, nor is it meant to be. Rather, it is the unusual formality of the situation—the men being properly identified and thanks being dutifully given—which makes for the drollery.

What has been revealed about the Mennonite people in their folklore rhymes—their closeness to the natural world, their emphasis upon homemaking virtues, their compassion, imagination, and wit—all are evident too (plus other characteristics) in their many maxims. This collection has more than 150 sayings so that they alone tell us much about the Mennonite way of life. But they are typical of sayings of almost any culture—close parallels will be found with some common in English.

Also typical is that several *Plautdietsch* maxims, as some in English again, give opposing views so that at least one of a pair will be appropriate no matter what the situation. For example, in English we say, "Look before you leap" as well as "He who hesitates is lost." In *Plautdietsch* we pair "*Jelenga, jeleewa*" (The longer, the better) with "*Jelenga, jeschlemma*" (The longer, the worse).

One group of sayings is "Maxims about Marriage and Raising Children." What is of interest, first of all, is not the emphasis on skills required by members of a normal family to make the family comfortable and happy—we come to expect that from Mennonites—but sayings dealing with special situations such as the death of a mother and/or the remarriage of the father and the effect it will have on the children. (Poor man!—in one of the maxims in question, the father becomes a blind fool.) For even in normal situations there are still problems, and note the humor supplied by these rural images: a husband can bring in money by the hayracksful, but the wife will soon spend it all by apronsful; when the rooster's away, the hen wants a full accounting.

Children, so the maxims say, are a blessing in a family, particularly when they are small. More than one set of parents in any age or culture would agree that "Little children press down on the lap" but that "Big children weigh much upon the heart." Mennonite parents, so their maxims say once more, must look to themselves if the children turn wayward. The responsibility of upbringing rests with the adults—they know best—and the sooner things are done the better—"What little Hans doesn't learn, big Hans never will."

What is learned includes habits of tidiness (cleaning up after meals) and deportment (girls' abstaining from whistling). Clumsiness must go, and limits must be obeyed. Actions have consequences; bad actions have

Operation of spinning wheel at Heritage Village.

Interior oven for baking and central heating at Heritage Village. Straw was one of the fuels. Note the covered cauldron built into the left side of the oven.

Mennonite *Faspa* table setting. *Faspa* (cognate word—"vesper") is a mid-afternoon snack. *Tweeback* or double buns are on a plate at the left.

bad consequences, involving parental punishment if needed. This maxim sums up the situation: "Bringing up children badly is not just a failing—it's a crime."

The "Maxims for Housewives" accentuate the old-fashioned role of women followed by a Mennonite homemaker. She is concerned with setting a good table, where bread is the staff of life. The *Plautdietsch* expression is forceful: "*Broot schleit de Hunga doot*" (Bread strikes the hunger dead"). But man does not live by bread alone, even literally at the table, and the wise homemaker sees that all foods are distinctive in flavor. The reader could note here that although Mennonites generally lived in their tight little communities, aloof from their other countrymen in their various homelands, the wives were quick to adopt national dishes into the culture. Thus Russian foods such as *Borscht* and *Wrennetje* have become traditional items on Mennonite bills of fare.

The homemaker is concerned also with appearances, and one maxim's reference to the colors red and green suggests that there was a liking for brightness and not just the sombre shades usually associated with Mennonite women's dress. The women knew, however, that outward appearances were not what really counted. There are three maxims to aver this point. One takes issue with the notion that clothes make the man; the other two suggest the absurdity of parading one's finery down the street when one's housekeeping at home is neglected.

The homemaker realizes that good management is the key to her work. She shops frugally, for is it not true that "Who buys what she doesn't need will soon need what she can't buy"? This Mennonite maxim has been stated in various ways by many economy-minded individuals, including Henry Thoreau in his classic *Walden*, 1854. The housewife wastes not and therefore wants not. An extra bit of waste cloth may serve for a future patch; leftovers in food can make a second meal. She so con-

trols her household environment that her family members will all say: "East, west— / Home is best."

The homemaker's husband has his own guidelines in *Plautdietsch*, the "Maxims for Farmers." Most of them have to do with weather. Birds and animals can be looked to in providing forecasts. A crowing rooster at evening signifies rain—but then again, according to a second maxim, maybe it does not. The actions of wild animals, blackbirds and wolves, are also looked to. Perhaps the color of the evening sky is the best portent of things to come.

And there are seasonal portents. Mennonites, like farmers everywhere, cannot live without hope so that to them, a maxim says, a cold winter presages a good harvest in the coming year. But weather to an olden-day farming people was as unpredictable as it often is to modern-day scientists: "April [still] / Does what it will." To the Mennonites, "On God's good tending / Is all now depending."

It was because of the unpredictability of weather that several maxims advise the farmer to "Gather ye Rosebuds while ye may,"[7] for, as one saying has it, "Weddings and good haying weather don't come every day." There was a sense of time hurrying on, of seasons relentlessly succeeding each other, no matter what man would do. A philosophical farmer could well take the attitude—all in good time, and seek pleasure in the work itself and not just the outcome: "Work makes life sweet."

A very large group of *Plautdietsch* sayings could be termed "Maxims about the Vicissitudes of Life." As might be expected, they are chiefly about life's misfortunes, setbacks, and disappointments (the "downs" of life as opposed to the "ups")—when things are going well, we do not need the solace or encouragement of age-old wisdom. An individual's luck can be so down, as one maxim affirms, that he does not have enough food left to entice a dog to come out of a hot oven. But it is really the long duration of any woe which makes for the burden. And where misfortune strikes, ridicule will be sure to follow.

Many of the maxims deal with the causes of the misfortunes. Some of the woes seem to be just a matter of circumstances, for that is the way of the world—one person has the purse, but someone else has the money. And that situation may not remain so. Luck is equated with glass: both break easily.

Woes may also stem from another person's action so that again it may not be possible to find an easy remedy. One maxim here specifically refers to that other person being the country's ruler. The Mennonites through their long history well knew the consequences to their people of a nation's inconsistent or wavering authority.

Most of the woes, according to the maxims, arise within the self—"Everyone makes his own destiny." There are references to such things as experience and age, although here the comment is hardly consolatory. True, one gains wisdom with age, but age itself is not without discomfort. Furthermore, the sensitivity needed to gain this wisdom makes one all the more subject to life's hurts. Having a brazen attitude, on the other hand, only sets one up to be knocked down—to have one's horns trimmed is the rural *Plautdietsch* image.

If one tries to cushion himself from these woes by accumulating material wealth, something the whole world "shrieks" for, then one must be prepared to rationalize the paradox—"Dressed-up and grumbly; ragged and happy." A Mennonite must needs seek ultimate solace in the maxim which states that "Man proposes / But God disposes." (The world's tribulations have come to be the *necessary* attributes of what John Keats in a letter describes as "The vale of Soul-making"[8] —or come to be akin to what George Herbert in his poem "The Pulley" calls the weariness that drives man to God.[9])

In consequence of such faith, there are some maxims which speak for acceptance of one's lot—to "... eat what is here / And drink what is clear." Even "A blind hen also finds a good kernel now and then." If it does not rain to produce that good kernel, why then the poor people can the better dry their shirts. There is just no point in making "A great big to-do / Over little to do."

On the other hand, several maxims speak for self-reliance, a mustering of one's forces to persist in spite of adversity. In fact, one of the maxims has a military image, unusual for a noncombative ethnic group: "Don't throw away your pistol in the trench." An equally colorful maxim advocating perseverance is—"We've got past the dog; now we still have to get past the tail." At such times, life's travail seems endless, says one maxim, but another affirms, in part, that everything has an end. Perhaps the best evidence of Mennonite perseverance is seen in the humor with which tribulation is met. For this maxim has a qualifying rider: yes, everything comes to an end—except a sausage. It comes to two ends!

A second very large group of *Plautdietsch* sayings are simply "Maxims about Daily Behavior." Some of them, in describing how to get a job done, are related to those previously discussed about perseverance. A job once started should be completed—"If at all, then all the way!" Meanwhile, a person has to know how to help himself, says one maxim, for another affirms that nothing comes from nothing.

Once a job is started, it is half done. And it is the steady application of hard work that spells success, never merely talking about the project: "It helps nothing just to pucker the lips; you have to whistle." But the "whistling" should be done with some forethought (only the catching of fleas needs be done with haste). Otherwise, the person realizes to his chagrin the truth of this maxim: "Who doesn't use his head must use his feet."

Among the olden-day Mennonites, there was always some ambivalence about using one's head to gain knowledge explicitly, however. They were among the first group of people, as has previously been mentioned, to insist that all its members receive a *basic* education. And yet many adult members subscribed to the maxim —"The more school, the more fool."

Perhaps there was a religious explanation, a Biblical reference that colored Mennonite thinking with regard to acquiring knowledge. Their corresponding adage for "Curiosity killed the cat" is "Curiosity has spoiled the world." The action has been completed in the past, and the effect is universal. If the past extends back to the beginnings of time, then the maxim seems to stem from the Genesis story of Eve's tasting fruit from the tree of knowledge. The Mennonites had always lived a simple life, and that simplicity could be applied to schooling as well, in order to save a person from coming to some unknown grief.

The best education, after all, was in the familiar world of house and byre, field and pasture. It was a practical, lifelong thing where "Doing mean[t] learning," where even "A tree [was] never too old to bend" (cf. an opposite view, though: "You can't teach an old dog to bark"). Such experience or such learning might not come easily either, but there was a maxim to mollify setbacks: "There is no shame in falling down, only in staying there." The experiences were part of a rich, full life—"Youthful actions, old reflections."

A significant part of any education is learning the amenities of everyday living, those things which give grace to one's actions. Several of them find expression in Mennonite folklore. A random selection includes— "With his hat in his hand / Man's welcome throughout the land"; "Wounds from words are hard to heal"; "The wisest gives in [in an argument]"; "Who gives willingly, gives doubly." A person whose life is not guided by these sayings will find, according to two other maxims, that his character has great need of being trimmed down with a plane or a grindstone.

Finally the maxims about daily behavior give a lot of practical advice on a variety of subjects. A rural image is used to speak about knowing one's place when we are told that a *horse* knows its own crib. Another farm animal appears in an aphorism, equally vivid, which promotes individual initiative. The saying is of further interest because the same expression is found in a Chinese proverb: "He's waiting for geese, already roasted, to fly into his mouth." A second saying on the same subject is also of interest, not because it has a counterpart in English (as we have seen, many *Plautdietsch* maxims do) but because it is, untypically, not as concrete as the English version. Whereas the English say that the early bird catches the worm, the Mennonites say only that he who rises early will make something of himself.

And here are some other *Plautdietsch* maxims about daily behavior which will sound familiar when translated into English. "One shouldn't buy a cat in a sack." "He's made his own bed; now he must sleep in it" (there is also a second version about stirring up one's own *Mooss*, now having to eat it). "Who lives dangerously dies dangerously." "A little too late is much too late."

Whatever the maxim, however insignificant its few words seemed, it encapsulated some truth about human existence so that its applicability was ever fresh and its very economy of words made it memorable through succeeding generations. Perhaps the substance of one last maxim, even though another meaning is intended, may be a comment on the value we should give to all these little bits of folklore: "Who holds the little of no worth / Is never worthy of the great."

This collection contains three additional sections of bits of folklore ("Comparisons," "Other Expressions," and "One-Word Characterizations"). In the first of these, the *Plautdietsch* "Comparisons," there are also some clichéd similes, as in English (for example, cold as ice, white as snow), but they are not included here. What is collected are the unique comparisons, many dealing with people and occupations which were part of the Mennonite way of life in the rural villages—or with animals which these people saw or tended during their daily round of activities.

Traditionally Mennonites have been a farming people, but their self-sufficient communal life dictated that each husbandman also engage in one particular trade contributing to the smooth operation of the village, as has been mentioned in a previous section. Thus a farmer might also be a tailor, scissors grinder, or carpenter. Similes involving these trades would not then be unusual. Looking at one example—"... talks like a tailor"—we might think, at first glance, that it does not seem particularly apt, until we think of the man's scissors busily snipping away, opening and shutting like someone's mouth in conversation.

Most of the colorful comparisons have to do with animals. There are ones about stubborn horses, stupid cows, and sausage-stealing cats—familiar enough in the Mennonite world. The comparisons are always applied to some person. At times there is an ironic component so that if someone "has as much freedom as a dog in a well," we know he has no freedom at all. Or if something "fits like a saddle on a sow," we know just how inappropriate or unbecoming it is.

Similes give emphasis to any statement in one way or another. In *Plautdietsch* folklore we have these examples: "handy as a crank on an overcoat"; "monotonous as a buttermilk tune"; and "crazy as beanstalks." If someone "keeps turning like a windmill" (a characteristic image of the Dutch Mennonites), we can see he thinks overly much of his fine appearance and in displaying it. If he "sits there like a duck on a stump," he does not know which way to turn. And if he "lives like a maggot in lard," he has finally achieved perfect happiness.

There are many "Other Expressions" which could not be omitted from this collection. They deal with a person's physical appearance, his mental acuity, and his emotions and the exclamations which verbalize them.

Many more expressions are about the mental attributes than about the physical ones, however. Perhaps one's bodily make-up was just not a serious concern, as evidenced by this expression: "Short-and-fat's not much for shape, but sense there's none in tall-and-thin."

The *Plautdietsch* language has different ways of describing an intelligent person: he knows which end of the handle the fork is on, he will not be sold a pair of glasses, and he has not fallen on his head. If he has a nail in his head, though, then he is a know-it-all and no better than the very stupid. The dense person is characterized by having a loose spoke or by having been bitten by a cow. Disparaging remarks are also made about the squeamish, who eat with long teeth, and the thoroughly disagreeable, with whom one cannot even eat noodles. Those kinds of individuals, of whatever intelligence, are best given anything the chickens lay, except the eggs—that is, nothing at all.

It is only in tabulating all the expressions that one realizes how many describe a situation where individuals are at wits' end. Who knows?—there may well be some tie-in with the persecution and restrictions endured by the Mennonites through the centuries while they lived in Europe. A person may be piping out of the last hole, with not enough food to fill a hollow tooth—not even salt for an egg, his bowl broken, and his oxen at the foot of a hill. So say five separate expressions, and there may be a dozen similar ones.

Reactions to trying situations may take several forms. There can be a boiling over of one's gall in anger. Then a person with "hair on his teeth" may want to see the antagonist "under four eyes" (a direct face-to-face confrontation). This is one way of carrying out *Rosmack* (cleaning house metaphorically)! But that may only give a "tomcat dance" (stir up a hornets' nest). Things get "out of bounds and bonds," and the Mennonite way is otherwise. It is better to record the incident "on the chimney" (to drop the matter).

"When all ropes tear" (everything goes to pieces), so

begins another expression, at least then one has peace, for the affair is past worrying about. Other expressions confirm that all that is really needed is a *Krupunja* (a roof to crawl under) and a *Fiastäd* (farmstead, a permanent place of fire or hearth). In time, the person will find that things will again "bite his belly" (make him laugh), and oats will "prick" him. A stone will have fallen "off his heart." *Mein (T)seit*—yes!

The final section of folklore in this book consists of the shortest items of all—"One-Word Characterizations." The English language has them too, words such as "sad-sack" and "buffoon," but *Plautdietsch* seems to be overflowing with examples of this sort of nomenclature. It is probably part of Mennonite humor that there are so many, that no individual, whatever his character, can escape from being tagged with some one-word description which generally is amusingly uncomplimentary. Also, the Mennonite people have always been quick to bestow nicknames upon each other (their real Christian names were a few Biblical names used over and over, creating confusion in identification), and the one-word characterizations seem to be another aspect of the same propensity.

There are descriptions of children, particularly misbehaved children, but most of the designations are terms to be used in an affectionate manner, such as *Piepe-dakjsel* (pipe-lid) and *Koddajalaups* (ragged dolt). An older child or youth might be termed a *Junga-schnääkja* (young whippersnapper). There are relatively few designations reserved for women (it seems that their traditional and well-defined homemaking role did not admit of much variation in behavior), but the ones we have are blunt enough. She could be termed a *Struckhakjs* (brush-witch), a *Klotjedroaga* (rumor-monger), or a *Kjrät* (toad, a word once applied to lowlanders).

Most of the one-word characterizations pertain to men. Their outdoor work—often in association with neighbors, as were their business dealings—gave them full opportunity to exhibit a wide range of behavior and so earn a variety of epithets. There was a clever man (*Näajen-klooka*—nine-wiseman) and a stupid one (*Dwautsch*). There was an able man (*Dusent-Kjensla*—thousand-performer) and an unable one (*Schlosäwen-doot*—slay-seven-dead). The able man might well be put upon, and then he would become a *Nootnoagel* (need-nail). The inability of the other person might stem from many causes—laziness, slovenliness, slowness, indecisiveness—all of which had their characteristic tags. The indecisive person, for instance, might be a "soft-bread" or a "stocking."

Kjeadel was the term for a stalwart person, a likable character.[10] In *Plautdietsch* there are many, many times the number of terms for unlikable characters. They might be "drink-bumps" (drunkards), "wooden-shoe captains" (officious individuals), or "intestine-fevers" (pests who give one a pain). Several epithets referred to part of the anatomy in a compound word, with *Kopp* (head) being the most common noun so incorporated, preceded by a great variety of qualifiers. Thus there were "thickheads," "mudheads," "tinheads," "cottage-cheeseheads"—to name just a few.

Other parts of the anatomy prominently featured in one-word characterizations were throats, teeth, and mouths—because, it seems, they have to do with the very act of expression by which people tend to distinguish themselves from others. With usage of the word "mouth," there was often some built-in humor among the Mennonites. The *Plautdietsch* language has separate words for a human mouth (*Mul*) and an animal's mouth (*Frät*). Then to be a *Plaupamul* (prattle-mouth) was bad enough, but to be a *Blaubafrät* (blabbermouth) was much worse. Again, as in so much Mennonite *Plautdietsch* folklore, the expressions are ever colorful; indeed, the terms "sensuous" and "kinesthetic," referred to at the beginning of this analysis of the folklore, are usually applicable.

This analysis has gone from nursery rhymes and games, to songs and riddles, to maxims and other short items of the Western Canadian Mennonites' folklore. The coverage has been broad, but the examination, while it has tried to be thorough, has not been exhaustive—principally because of the wealth of the material. The collection itself in this book is by no means exhaustive, although it represents, it is hoped, a good start in assembling examples of this interesting literature which could not be put off for another generation.

The various items here, to be personal, I have learned for the most part from my mother—at my mother's knee, as it were. She learned them chiefly from her mother, who hailed from the Molochnaya colony in Russia. But my mother learned some also from her father who was born in the Chortitza colony there. Thus my inheritance of material comes from the two parent colonies which the Mennonites founded when they left their previous homeland in Poland-Prussia. Some rhymes too come from my father, and others have been contributed by friends, who learned them from *their* parents or from *their* friends. For such is the typical dispersion of folklore.

In providing the English translations—and here I am referring particularly to what I have called the "bits" of folklore—I have given meanings which these items had when spoken in our family. I realize that in a few instances a certain *Plautdietsch* expression may have held a somewhat different meaning when used by another Mennonite family. Comment has been made earlier on the manifold interpretation characteristic of folklore. Such additional meanings, where they do exist, can only increase the richness of the folklore presented. Certainly, the *Plautdietsch* folklore of the Western Canadian Mennonites is already a rich body of literature.

FOUR

Some Thoughts on *Plautdietsch* Orthography

Arnold Dyck, composing his "Koop enn Bua opp Reise" series of humorous stories in the 1930s and 1940s, was foremost among authors in popularizing *Plautdietsch* as a written form of expression.[1] Till then it had been for all practical purposes a *spoken* language only, with no standardized system of spelling. Dyck based his orthography, one which he continued to refine throughout his life, on the Molochnaya dialect of the language (stemming from the speech used in the Molochnaya colony of Mennonites in Russia), which seemed for him to be the standard to follow. Another popularizer of *Plautdietsch* as a literary vehicle, this time on recordings as well as in writing, is Reuben Epp, whose first works were published in the early 1970s.[2] He also worked in the Molochnaya dialect and developed his own orthography accordingly.[3]

When in 1975 I began to collect the material in this anthology, the first task I set myself was to devise a simplified orthography for personal use in recording each item as I heard it. As a matter of circumstances, I too based my system on the Molochnaya speech of my forebears: my maternal grandmother was born in that colony in Russia, and it was from her that my mother learned to speak, just as I later learned from *my* mother.

Thus I said *blauw* (blue) and *grauw* (gray), using the vowel sound *au* in Molochnaya fashion (see the "Key to *Plautdietsch* Pronunciation"), instead of the *bleiw* and *greiw* of Old Colony speech (as spoken in Chortitza, the oldest Mennonite colony in Russia).[4] I also said *hooch* (high) and *Oog* (eye) instead of *huach* and *Uag.* But for Grandmother's original *koke* (to cook) and *moke* (to make), I now said *koake* and *moake*, as she later came to say the words. This was a compromise pronunciation, for the Old Colonists said *käake* and *mäake*. The Old Colonists also retained *n*-endings to many words (see the "Key" again) so that an extreme example might read: *Ons Doften saut aul lang oppem Boggen toom no Oomtje Friesen foaren Tänen ut rieten loten* (Our Dave sat already long on the buggy for to Mr. Friesen to drive, teeth out to pull let). A Molochnaya spokesman would drop the final *n*'s, including the one in the surname.

I have included these examples here not only to illustrate the dialect which forms the basis of the orthography used in this book but also to give the reader a glimpse of some of the difficulties in devising a standardized spelling for the *Plautdietsch* language. The spelling depends upon how words are said, and yet this language, because of its different dialects,[5] has different ways of saying the same words. Even where a certain word may be said identically by two people, a third and fourth person may still *hear* it differently. An acceptable spelling system must somehow allow for regional differences in pronunciation while still employing a set standard of symbols. And the simpler a spelling system can be, the more easily the readers can become used to it. (Of course, any system, when one is acquainted with it, seems to be the right one, and a new system always requires some time before one "takes" to it.)

In April, 1982, scholars of Mennonite *Plautdietsch* assembled at the University of Winnipeg to make a fresh attempt at developing a "standard" system of spelling the *Plautdietsch* language. The system was to be kept as phonetic as possible. Altogether, fifteen individuals under Chairman Al Reimer took part in this one-day seminar to arrive at a workable consensus. The Manitoba Mennonite Historical Society, the Mennonite Literary Society, and the Chair of Mennonite Studies at the university sponsored the event.[6]

In the past, systems of *Plautdietsch* orthography relied to a large extent upon German as a guide in the spelling of words, that is, adopting a High German system of spelling for a Low German language. There was some justification for this. German was the *written* language of the Western Canadian Mennonites for the century immediately preceding their emigration to America from Russia. Such spelling was familiar to them from their own religious literature and their newspapers printed in the German language. German, after all, was one of Europe's best known languages—second only to Russian in the extent of its use there.

What seemed apt some years ago, however, might not necessarily be so apparent in the 1980s—particularly as it would pertain to an anthology of folklore which was collected not just for Mennonites but for the general reading public. Even among the Mennonites of Western Canada, many no longer can write (High) German and so are not acquainted with *its* orthography. Further-

more, an undue reliance upon the German system of spelling in writing the Mennonites' homely *Plautdietsch* seems to ignore the fact that for most of this people's existence, the first two-and-a-half centuries, their written language was Dutch, more akin to *Plautdietsch* than (High) German is, in its also being a Low German tongue. It was this close kinship which made for the ready adoption of *Plautdietsch* by the Mennonites when they first steadfastly resisted the use of German.

In counter-argument, the "tradition" of writing *Plautdietsch* in Western Canada (albeit one that stems from just this century) cannot be ignored either. Its existence alone becomes a force, whatever new expertise there may be, affecting future decisions. The result was that the Winnipeg committee of 1982, having in attendance individuals who had themselves with much thought already devised spelling systems, chose to select the best features of these systems and those of past ones. They were combined in a rationalized orthography which could readily be adopted by all future writers of *Plautdietsch*.

This anthology of folklore uses this new standardized orthography. "The new system," Al Reimer has stated, "is flexible enough to allow for some minor orthographic variations in rendering certain sounds."[7] According to the editors of *A Sackful of Plautdietsch*, 1983, such flexibility "can only add richness and texture to the *Plautdietsch*."[8] In *The Windmill Turning*, the variations are indeed minor, the only real one involving the *kj/tj* sound.

For the uninitiated, the *k* sound in *Plautdietsch* has been palatalized in many words to *kj*, for example, *Kjätel* (kettle)—compare Dutch *ketel* or German *Kessel*. (A related palatalization has occurred in some English words: "kirk" becoming "church.") To Old Colony speakers, this sound is pronounced as a definite *kj* (*k* blended to an English *y* as in "cue" or "cube"). But to most Molochnaya speakers, the sound is probably more accurately described or transliterated as *tj*.[9] Which consonant cluster should be used? The Winnipeg committee wrestled with this controversy and came to a compromise solution, to use *kj* for an initial sound in words, but *-tj* for medial and final sounds.

The compromise has perhaps not completely satisfied either group and so not proved wholly acceptable. Thus committee member Herman Rempel, in revising his Mennonite Low German dictionary under the sponsorship of the Mennonite Literary Society, has used the *kj* spelling throughout in all affected words, thus giving this work an Old Colony orientation.[10] It can be argued that the Old Colony Mennonites "preserved the original Low German in its purest form"[11] because they had been the first group to leave Poland-Prussia; therefore their pronunciation should be given weight.

Be that as it may, I have chosen to use *kj* throughout as well, despite my own Molochnaya linguistic ties (and realizing that the knowledgeable reader is free to pronounce words involving *kj/tj* as he is accustomed to). My reason for doing so is what I call the *kj*'s "visual verisimilitude," its closer resemblance on the page not only to the original word source but also to cognate words in Dutch, German, *or* English. The *kj* usage thus facilitates ease of reading. For example, "fork" in *Plautdietsch* is spelled *Forkj* (not *Fortj*); "milk" is spelled *Malkj* (not *Maltj*). Also, the *Plautdietsch* word for "I," as spelled here, is *ekj*. This relates nicely to the Dutch *ik* and the German *ich*—but a reader can still say it with a *-tj* ending if that is his wont.[12]

Related diminutive endings—so common in *Plautdietsch*, as they are in Dutch—are another matter. Here I use the *-tje* form, in keeping with my Molochnaya kin (and the 1982 Winnipeg committee), but for similar reasons as my opting for the *kj* usage above. The *-tje* form is that used by the Mennonites' Dutch forebears and so is identical with the source. Furthermore, its distinct form serves purposely to separate it from those *kj*'s which appear in regular word endings and so avoid possible confusion. Thus *hoakje* means "to rake," while *Hoatje*

means "little heart" (*Hoat* is "heart"). Again, such usage makes for ease of reading. Futher examples of its usage include *Kjiel—Kjieltje* (wedge—little wedge, a kind of noodle) and *Stool—Stooltje* (chair—little chair); also words of diminutive-*like* endings: *Hoftje* (hawk). It might be that this kind of separate function of *kj* and *tj* is the compromise that will be most workable.[13]

To readers who are unacquainted with (or have forgotten) *Plautdietsch*, a few explanations will help in their understanding of the "Key to *Plautdietsch* Pronunciation" which follows, even though it embodies the new standardized orthography. With the vowels, a reader should note that they are, of course, usually not exactly alike in different languages. At the same time the sounds are not so unlike that a speaker cannot get by, by saying the English equivalents. After all, there are different dialects within the *Plautdietsch* itself.

One vowel which needs some attention is the *Plautdietsch* long *u* (that is, a final *u*, or *u* followed by a single consonant). While Molochnaya speakers may say it much as in English, people with Old Colony roots pronounce it with the front part of the mouth, differently from the rounded sound of the English vowel in, for example, "pool." Other final vowels to note are *a* and *e*. Final *-a* (pronounced *ah*) represents a lapsed "-er" ending and is found in words like *Shusta* (shoester) and also in many words as part of a modified vowel: *Däa* (door), *hia* (here), *Boa* (bear), *sua* (sour). Final *-e* (like an *uh*) is always pronounced (as it is in Chaucer). While a final *-e* occurs in a variety of words, it is also the infinitive ending of verbs (with Old Colonists here using the *-en*), and the substitution of *-a* for the *-e* can, in many instances, change the verb or action word into the noun representing the doer of that act. Thus *äte* means "to eat," and *Äta* is the "eater" himself.

There are two pairs of additional vowel sounds that do warrant some special discussion for English readers because the distinction within each pair appears to be important chiefly in *Plautdietsch* alone. The sounds in questions are all said in English, but dictionaries tend to treat each pair of sounds as a single diphthong. The two pairs are represented in this *Plautdietsch* orthography by *au* and *oo* and by *ei* and *ee*.

The *au* sound is fully rounded, while *oo* is said with the tongue brought slightly forward (compare the two English words "how" and "house" respectively to hear the difference). Similarly *ei* is more rounded than *ee* (again compare English "sigh" with "sight" for the difference). With these distinctions in mind, we can differentiate between such *Plautdietsch* words as *daut* (that) and *doot* (dead) or *Blaut* (blade or leaf) and *Bloot* (blood); also *Hei* (hay) and *hee* (he) or *Weit* (wheat) and *weet* (knows).

The *ee* sound can also occur in the *Plautdietsch* word for the definite article "the." In English, "the" is pronounced *thə* unstressed, and *thē* stressed. A similar situation obtains in *Plautdietsch*, where the article is *de* unstressed, and *dee* stressed (the latter form is used more than its English counterpart and is more or less synonymous with "that"). Here these letter representations are also the correct spellings since the orthography tries to be as phonetic as it can. There are then not only two spellings for "the," but the matter is further complicated by the use of case endings and by the use of the *dee*-form as a kind of personal pronoun (see the Appendix). (Note that the indefinite article form, *e(e)n*, is also used for the indefinite pronoun, "one"—again see the Appendix.)

Little need here be said in this system of orthography about the consonants. English readers, however, may need to be reminded about the usage of *d* and *j*. Unlike the practice in Dutch and German, final *d*'s are pronounced as *d* and not as *t*. The reason for doing so is simply that *Plautdietsch* is unique among these three languages in having many words ending in fact with a *d*-sound. Examples are *lud* (loud) and *Bad* (bed). *Plautdietsch j*'s are always pronounced as *y*'s, but then that is

true in many languages. When *j* is combined with *ch* (*jch*) or with *g*, *k*, or *n* (*gj*, *kj*, *nj*), it softens or flattens the sound, as explained in the "Key."

Some problems do arise with the letter *s*. Before a vowel, or as a single final *s* that is part of an accented syllable but not following *l*, it is usually a voiced sibilant (like an English *z*). Without these restrictions, or before a consonant, or as a medial or final double-*s*, it is unvoiced or whispered (a hard *s* as in most English words). (Of course, a final *s* preceded by *f*, *k* or *kj*, *p*, or *t* is always hard because of the consonant's effect in combination.) Examples are provided in the "Key," but there are exceptions. They occur because the orthography is not completely a "one sound—one symbol" concept—mainly because there are short and long *o*'s and *u*'s, depending upon the number of following consonants. One consonant makes for a long vowel, two consonants for a short one.

Regarding these vowels and the letter *s*, the reader can envision situations where a short *o*, for instance, might be required (necessitating *two s*'s, as just explained), followed by a voiced sibilant (symbolized by but a *single s*). Then arbitrary decisions must be made. As a result we have these sample spellings: *Kos* (goat), *Fos* (fuzz)—short *o*, voiced *s*; *Os* (carrion), *Spos* (fun)— long *o*, unvoiced *s*. Similar exceptions occur with the letter *u*: *Kuckerus* (corn)—short *u*, voiced *s*; *Hus* (house), *Lus* (louse), *Mus* (mouse), *tus* (at home)—all long *u*, unvoiced *s*. Note that a few exceptions also occur where these vowels remain long despite the presence of two following consonants; for example, *schrots* (slanty) or *junt* (yours) and also *puste* (to blow). (Where verbs are concerned, long vowels will remain so despite verbal endings of person or tense.)

An additional problem with the letter *s* in *Plautdietsch* is that Old Colony speakers pronounce an initial *s* in many words as unvoiced even though there is a following vowel. Examples are *Socka* (sugar) and *Sieropp* (syrup). Molochnaya speakers use a *ts*-sound here.

Where such words occur in the book, a compromise *(t)s* spelling is used.

Apart from these concerns with some of the vowels and consonants, the "Key" is self-explanatory. English readers may notice from it that many unusual spellings in their own language date from its Germanic origins. Thus in "knight" the *k* and *gh* used to be distinctly said in denoting this hireling in the feudal system. In *Plautdietsch* today the cognate word, pronounced *Kjnajcht*, is still used to denote a hired man (see the Appendix for other interesting cognates). People perusing this book should see many similarities between *Plautdietsch* and English and so gain a deeper understanding of their own language.

It is hoped that for all readers of this book—whether they give particular attention to the mechanics of the *Plautdietsch* language, or to the rich history of the Western Canadian Mennonites, or to the principal focus of this work, the folklore itself—the material presented here will enhance their appreciation of the Mennonite presence in the Canadian cultural mosaic. May the readers be not only enlightened, but entertained many times over.

KEY TO PLAUTDIETSCH
PRONUNCIATION

Letter Representation	Example (translation)	Approximate Sound in English
a	fat (fat)	father
ä	nä (no)	brae
äa	näajen (nine)	fair
au	Faut (vat)	bough, landau
e (followed by two consonants)	ess (is)	bedding
e (final)	kome (come)	open
ea	weare (were)	ear
ee	twee (two)	night
ei	twei (broken)	nigh
i (followed by two consonants)	witt (white)	kitten
ia	Fia (fire)	Via Rail
ie	mien (mine)	field
o when followed by two consonants*	Botta (butter)	but, sonny
o when followed by only one or none*	lot (late), jo (yes)	note, go
oa	Koa (car)	boa
oo	Foot (foot)	bout
u when followed by two consonants*	Buddel (bottle)	pudding
u when followed by only one or none*	ut (out), nu (now)	rule, jujitsu
ua	Stua (store)	suable

*There are exceptions: see the preceding explanation, p. 39.

CONSONANTS

NOTE: *Plautdietsch* consonants, including their combinations, are pronounced as they are in English, but with the following exceptions. Note too that consonants here are doubled after the one-letter vowels *e, i,* and short *o* and short *u*—for example, *Schepp* (ship), *rikj* (rich), *Oss* (ox), and *Trubbel* (trouble)—but not after the prefix *je-*.

Letter Representation	Example (translation)	Explanation
ch	Krach (crash)	the whispered sound of *ch* in Scottish *loch*. (Note that a *k* is always used for a hard *c* sound. When it needs to be doubled after a vowel, then *ck* is used.)
gj	Rigje (back, backbone)	a blend of English *g* + *y*.
j	jäl (yellow)	always like English *y*.
jch	Wajch (way, road) dijcht (watertight)	a blend of English *y* + *ch*, as above.
kj	Kjees (cheese) Forkj (fork)	a blend of English *k* + *y*.
n	halpe (to help) see halpe (they help) habe jeholpe (have helped) Laumpe (lamps)	final *n*'s are not retained here in pronunciation or spelling in these forms—infinitives, plural or past participle verbs, or some plural nouns. (Old Colony Mennonites do retain them.)
ng	Hunga (hunger)	as in "singer," never as in "finger."
nj	sinje (to sing)	a blend of English *n* + *y*.
r	Broot (bread)	always trilled.
s singly before vowels, or usually as a single final s in accented syllable not preceded by l*	säwen (seven) Jans (geese)	like English *z*.
s without above restrictions	Post (post) aules (all) Pels (fur coat)	unvoiced *s*.
ss	Bassem (broom) Sanss (scythe)	unvoiced *s*.
sch	schoap (sharp)	like English *sh*.
sp	Spoa (spoor)	at beginning of word or of part of compound word, then like *shp*.
st	Steen (stone)	at beginning of word or of part of compound word, then like *sht*.
(t)s	(T)soagel (tail)	a blend of *t* + unvoiced *s*, or omit the *t*.
tj**	Mustje (little mouse)	a blend of English *t* + *y*.
tsch	Pitsch (whip)	like *ch* in "chimney."
w	Wast (vest)	like English *v*.
zh	ruzhe (to make a rushing sound)	like *s* in "pleasure."
q, v, x, y	— (not used in *Plautdietsch*) —	

*See the preceding explanation, p. 39 for some exceptions. Note that a final s in combination with f, k or kj, p, or t will necessarily be unvoiced: *Blaufs* (bluing), *Knacks* (crack), *Akjs* (axe), *Bumps* (thud), *duts* (dozen).

**The cluster *tje* is the common diminutive ending in *Plautdietsch* (see the Appendix).

NOTES

1. A Unique History

1. They came from what the eminent biographer and popular historian André Maurois calls "the Frisian marshlands and the great coastal plains." See his book, *The Miracle of England* (New York: Garden City, 1940), p. 25.
2. Gerhard Lohrenz, *The Mennonites of Western Canada* (Winnipeg: n.p., 1974), p. 5.
3. Lohrenz, *The Mennonites of Western Canada*, p. 5.
4. Frank Harder, "Who Am I?" in Julius G. Toews and Lawrence Klippenstein, eds., *Manitoba Mennonite Memories* (Altona and Steinbach: Manitoba Mennonite Centennial Committee, 1974), p. 5. See also C. Henry Smith, *The Story of the Mennonites*, 5th edn., rev. Cornelius Krahn (Newton, Kans.: Faith and Life Press, 1981), pp. 172–73.
5. This famous passage from Alfred, Lord Tennyson is very apt here. See *The Complete Works of Tennyson*, Cambridge edn., ed. W. J. Rolfe (Boston: Houghton Mifflin, 1898), p. 89. The quotation is the final line (1. 70) of "Ulysses."
6. For a discussion of this problem as it related to Saskatchewan, see Adolf Ens, "The Public School Crisis Among Mennonites in Saskatchewan 1916–25," in Harry Loewen, ed., *Mennonite Images: Historical, Cultural, and Literary Essays Dealing with Mennonite Issues* (Winnipeg: Hyperion Press, 1980), pp. 73–81.
7. Lohrenz, *The Mennonites of Western Canada*, p. 12.
8. See Smith, *The Story of the Mennonites*, pp. 305–7, for further details on this point.
9. The enormity of these times is described more fully in Smith, *The Story of the Mennonites*, pp. 314–15. A book dealing with the perpetrators of these heinous acts is Victor Peters's *Nestor Makhno, The Life of an Anarchist* (Winnipeg: Echo Books, 1970). For a personal account see Gerhard Lohrenz, *Storm Tossed* (Winnipeg: Christian Press, 1976), pp. 88–95. Several novels in English have focused, or focused in part, upon this period of Mennonite history, including Rudy Wiebe's *The Blue Mountains of China* (Toronto: McClelland and Stewart, 1970); Barbara Claassen Smucker's *Days of Terror* (Toronto: Clarke Irwin, 1979); and Al Reimer's *My Harp Is Turned to Mourning* (Winnipeg: Hyperion Press, 1986).
10. *The Works of Thomas Gray*, 4 vols., ed. Edmund Gosse (New York: AMS Press, 1968), Vol. I, p. 77. The quotation is from line 75 of "Elegy written in a Country Church-Yard."
11. Lohrenz, *The Mennonites of Western Canada*, p. 29.

2. A Distinct Language

1. The reader is also referred to a short, scholarly treatment of the subject, "History of Mennonite *Plautdietsch*." It is one of the introductory essays, pages 11–18, in Al Reimer, Anne Reimer, and Jack Thiessen, eds., *A Sackful of Plautdietsch* (Winnipeg: Hyperion Press, 1983). Two much earlier articles speak of the significance of *Plautdietsch* as a distinct language: J. John Friesen, "Romance of Low German," *Mennonite Life*, II (April, 1947), 22–23, 47; and J. W. Goerzen, "'Plautdietsch' and English," *Mennonite Life*, VII (January, 1952), 18–19. Goerzen's doctoral dissertation as well is on this subject: "Low German in Canada, a Study of 'Plautdietsch' as Spoken by Mennonite Immigrants from Russia" (University of Toronto, 1952).
2. Paul Hiebert, *Doubting Castle* (Winnipeg: Queenston House, 1976), p. 36. Hiebert's tribute here to *Plautdietsch* is well worth quoting: "It is a lovely language, simple and to the point and much like English, differing from that convoluted High German...."
3. This would be the *Biestkens Bible*, which Nikolaes Biestkens in Emden had first published for the Mennonites

in 1560. It was the first Dutch Bible to be printed with paragraph divisions.

4. H. Leonard Sawatzky, "The Mennonites in Manitoba," in Julius G. Toews and Lawrence Klippenstein, eds., *Manitoba Mennonite Memories* (Altona and Steinbach: Manitoba Mennonite Centennial Committee, 1974), p. 15. The editors point out, page 11, that this article "is extracted from an invited paper presented by Prof. Sawatzky at the Ethnic Symposium of the Learned Societies of Canada in June 1970 entitled 'The Viability of Ethnic Group Settlement with Specific Reference to the Mennonite Reserves in Manitoba.'"

5. Cornelius Krahn, "Plattdeutsch (Plautdietsch)," in *The Mennonite Encyclopedia*, 4 vols. (Scottdale, Pa.: Mennonite Publishing House, 1955–59), Vol. IV, p. 186, uses the word "water," for example, to show that English, Dutch, and *Plautdietsch* are in some respects more similar than are *Plautdietsch* and German: the Dutch and *Plautdietsch* people say *water* and *Wota* respectively, while Germans say *Wasser*.

6. Lohrenz, *The Mennonites of Western Canada*, p. 29.

7. Julius G. Toews, "We Spoke English to the Horses and Low German to the Cows," in Toews and Klippenstein, eds., *Manitoba Mennonite Memories*, pp. 96–98.

8. Of course, during the beginnings of Mennonitism at the time of the Reformation, the lowlands were part of the Holy Roman Empire (Germany, in essence), but national identification had less meaning then than now, and loyalties were largely tribal—Frisian, Flemish, and so on. When the Vistula delta fell under Prussian domination, centuries later, our Mennonite ancestors soon left for Russia, as explained in the previous chapter.

9. John C. Wenger, "Mennonites," in *The Encyclopedia Americana*, 30 vols. (Danbury, Conn.: Grolier, 1983), Vol. XVIII, pp. 695–96.

10. Gabrielle Roy, *Garden in the Wind*, trans. Alan Brown (Toronto: McClelland and Stewart, 1977), p. 110.

11. Sawatzky, "The Mennonites in Manitoba," in Toews and Klippenstein, eds., *Manitoba Mennonite Memories*, p. 15.

12. A few families went so far as to think that the speaking of *Plautdietsch* was a morally inferior activity.

13. Fuller references are given in the bibliography. Note that a sample of Fritz Senn's *Plautdietsch* poems may be found in Reimer, Reimer, and Thiessen, eds., *A Sackful of Plautdietsch*, pp. 168–74; that Jack Thiessen's work on a much-expanded edition of his dictionary is an ongoing project; and that Margaret Epp's first novel is *A Fountain Sealed*, 1965.

3. A Rich Folklore

1. The expression, of course, was made famous in Abraham Lincoln's Gettysburg Address, November 19, 1863. The *Plautdietsch* language is indeed *of* the people, for the Mennonites incorporated into it, as their everyday life demanded, various colorful words of Polish and Russian origin. See Gerhard Wiens, "Russian in Low German," *Mennonite Life*, XIII (April, 1958), 75–78; and Jack Thiessen, "Mennonite *Plautdietsch*—The Odyssey of a People," forthcoming.

2. *The Complete Poems of Carl Sandburg*, rev. edn. (New York: Harcourt Brace Jovanovich, 1970), p. 615. The quotation is from the concluding section of *The People, Yes*, 1936 (sec. 107, 1. 4).

3. See Dorothy Berliner Commins, *Lullabies of Many Lands* (New York: Harper, 1941).

4. A child with the name Isaak would not feel so lucky, however. See the rhyme, "Isaak, Sprisaak"—No. 6-23 (in Chapter 6).

5. The note following item No. 7-19 (in Chapter 7) explains the connection between rhyme and hymn.

6. See the note following song No. 9-5 (in Chapter 9). For a fuller explanation see also J. G. Toews, "Traditional Mennonite Pastimes," in Julius G. Toews and Lawrence Klippenstein, eds., *Manitoba Mennonite Memories* (Altona and Steinbach: Manitoba Mennonite Centennial Committee, 1974), pp. 292–95.

7. This much-quoted admonition, the opening line of Robert Herrick's lyric, "To the Virgins, to make much of Time," although Cavalier in tone, is still appropriate in a discussion of Mennonite maxims because of its epigrammatic quality. See *The Poetical Works of Robert Herrick*, ed. L. C. Martin (Oxford: Clarendon Press, 1956), p. 84.

8. *The Letters of John Keats, 1814–1821*, 2 vols., ed. Hyder Edward Rollins (Cambridge, Mass.: Harvard University Press, 1958), Vol. II, p. 102.

9. *The Works of George Herbert*, ed. F. E. Hutchinson (Oxford: Clarendon Press, 1941), pp. 159–60.

10. *Kjeadel* is a variation of "Karl" or "Carl," derived from "Charles" the Great (Charlemagne). It can mean simply, "man"—compare Chaucer's Miller in *The Canterbury*

Tales, described as "a stout carl for the nones" (l. 545). See *The Works of Geoffrey Chaucer*, 2nd edn., ed. F. N. Robinson (Boston: Houghton Mifflin, 1961), p. 22. The Mennonite boys serving in the *Forstei* (forestry service) in prerevolutionary Russia proudly referred to themselves as *Kjeadels*, that is, as real he-men.

4. SOME THOUGHTS ON PLAUTDIETSCH ORTHOGRAPHY

1. Dyck's stories are now available as the second volume of the new four-volume edition of his collected works: Arnold Dyck, *Koop enn Bua opp Reise . . .*, ed. Al Reimer (Winnipeg: Manitoba Mennonite Historical Society, 1986).
2. Reuben Epp, *Biem Aunsiedle* (record) (Winnipeg: R.E.C. Recordings, 1972); *Onse Lied Vetahle* (record) (Winnipeg: R.E.C. Recordings, 1973); and *Plautdietsche Schreftsteckja* (Steinbach, Man.: Derksen Printers, 1972).
3. Originators of other systems include J. H. Janzen (the first to write in *Plautdietsch*), J. W. Goerzen, Peter Fast, Jack Thiessen, and Herman Rempel. See Al Reimer, "There's now an 'official' way to write Low German," *Mennonite Mirror*, XI (June, 1982), 7.
4. While *blauw* and *grauw* may be a compromise pronunciation between Old Colony *bleiw* and *greiw* and the usual Molochnaya *blau* and *grau*, note that they are identical to that which is spoken in Dutch. For a scholarly discussion of Old Colony-Molochnaya variations, see Jack Thiessen, "A New Look at an Old Problem: Mennonite *Plautdietsch*," forthcoming.
5. Reuben Epp has dramatized these differences in his humorous play, "Dee Jebroakne Alboage." It is included in his book, *Plautdietsche Schreftsteckja*, pp. 110–16.
6. See Al Reimer, "There's now an 'official' way to write Low German," *Mennonite Mirror*, pp. 7–8.
7. Al Reimer, "Introduction" to Herman Rempel, *Kjenn Jie Noch Plautdietsch? A Mennonite Low German Dictionary* (Winnipeg: Mennonite Literary Society, 1984), p. vii.
8. Al Reimer, Anne Reimer, and Jack Thiessen, eds., *A Sackful of Plautdietsch*, p. 18.
9. There is another consideration regarding the *kj/tj* sound. This palatalization is generally more pronounced in Russlander speech than it is in the conversation of those Mennonites who immigrated to America some fifty years earlier (and of their descendants). A casual listener, unacquainted with *Plautdietsch*, may not even detect it in some of the words where it does occur in this latter speech—for example, in *Kjist* (chest) and *Kjnee* (knee).
10. See note 7 above.
11. Cornelius Krahn, "Plattdeutsch (Plautdietsch)," in *The Mennonite Encyclopedia*, Vol. IV, p. 187.
12. A further possible confusion is also avoided by spelling affected medial *k* sounds as *kj*, rather than as *tj*. If the *tj* were used for medial and final sounds while the *kj* were retained exclusively for word beginnings, one could then have the situation where a word might begin with *kj* (e.g., *Kjint*—child) but change its spelling when it became the second part of a compound word (e.g., *Groottjint*—grandchild).
13. There is one other spelling variation which I would have liked to use in *The Windmill Turning* but chose to adhere to the pattern devised at the Winnipeg meeting. This variation does not affect at all, or even appear to affect, how a word is pronounced: it is simply the writing of all nouns in lower case, as in Dutch, the Mennonites' ancestral language, and in English.

PART TWO

Plautdietsch
Folklore

Two translations are provided for each rhyme, as there are for all the rhyming items in this collection. The first translation is a word-by-word reading. It is true that some of the phrases are idiomatic and a "good" translation would use corresponding idioms in English. However, the course here is deliberately chosen to give the reader a better glimpse of the train of thought in *Plautdietsch* and a chance to see how close its vocabulary is to that of English (in this latter regard see also the list of Some Cognate Words in the Basic Vocabulary of the Appendix). Something may be lost in the second translation, but it is a smoother version which keeps in mind that the essence of nursery rhymes is their rhyme and metre. In some cases the precise meaning must be altered to achieve a rhyme or near rhyme, but care has been taken to try to retain the overall gist. With the later maxims, an equivalent saying may be included.

FIVE

Rhymes of the Homelands

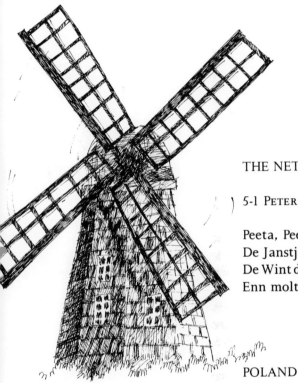

THE NETHERLANDS

5-1 PETER, PETER

Peeta, Peeta, komm mol äte;
De Janstjes schwame emm Wota;
De Wint dee dreit de Wintmäl romm
Enn molt daut Mäl fe Foda.

Peter, Peter, come once eat;
The little geese swim in the water;
The wind it turns the windmill
    round
And mills the flour for Father.

Peter, Peter, time for eating;
The goslings swim in the water;
The wind is turning the windmill
    round
And milling the grain for Father.

POLAND

5-2 KRUM, E-RUM

"Kromm, eromm,
Wua west du han?"
"Foda, ekj go no Pole."
"Kromm, eromm,
Waut west du doa?"
"Ekj well mie en Briegaum hole."

"Crooked, around,
Where want you thither?"
"Father, I go to Poland."
"Crooked, around,
What want you there?"
"I want me a bridegroom fetch."

"Krum, e-rum,
Where are you going?"
"Father, I go to Poland."
"Krum, e-rum,
Why are you going?"
"A bridegroom I want, you'll be
    knowing."

RUSSIA

5-3 STRAWBERRY, STRAWBERRY

Eadbäa, Eadbäa,
Komm no mie
Fief Kopietje
Jäw ekj die.

Strawberry, strawberry,
Come to me.
Five *kopecks*
Give I you.

Strawberry, strawberry,
Come to me.
Five new *kopecks*
I give to thee.

5-4 MARIE, MARIE

NOTE: *Kruschtje* are little pear-like fruit which grew in orchards on the Russian steppes. *Maruschtje* is a nonsense word.

Marie, Marie, maruschtje,
Jinkj emm Woolt no Kruschtje;
Kjeem de Rusche Steewel-kjnajcht
Enn neem ar aule Kruschtje wajch.

Marie, Marie, *maruschtje*,
Went in the woods for *Kruschtje*;
Came the Russian high-booted hired man
And took her all the *Kruschtje* away.

Marie, Marie, *maruschtje*,
Went to the woods for *Kruschtje*;
Came the Russian hired man
And took the little pears and ran.

5-5 How Will It End?

Woo soll et woare?—	How shall it be?—	How will it all end?—
De Kjinja roare,	The children cry,	The old doors creaking,
De Kjalwa bloare,	The calves bellow,	The small calves bleating,
De Däare knoare,	The doors creak,	The children crying,
De Russe foare,	The Russians drive,—	The Russians spying,—
Enn et rääjent!	And it rains!	And it rains!

AMERICA

5-6 Seeding-Time

De Wausch henjt oppem Tun—	The wash hangs on the fence—	The wash hangs on the fence—
Daut rääjent enn daut schniet;	It rains and it snows;	It's washed of all its grime;
De Jung-febiela sinjt:	The meadowlark sings:	The meadowlark still sings:
"Fief Doag bat Sodeltiet."	"Five days to saddle-time."	"Five days to seeding-time."

SIX

Nursery Rhymes

6-1 MILKING

Stripp, stripp, stroll,
Moakt dän Ama foll.

Strip, strip, strull,
Makes the pail full.

Strip, strip, strull,
Makes the milk-pail full.

6-2 SLEEP, WEE ONE, SLEEP

Schlop, Kjintje, schlop—
Bute senn de Schop,
Dee Schop mett witte Woll;
Kjintje, drinkj dien Buckje foll.

Sleep, little child, sleep—
Outside are the sheep,
The sheep with white wool;
Little child, drink your belly full.

Sleep, wee one, sleep—
Outside are the sheep,
The sheep with pure white wool;
Wee one, drink your belly full.

6-3 BUTTER, BUTTER

Botta, Botta,
Fonn eene Koo;
Jeet en Plumpstje
Wota too.

Butter, butter,
From one cow;
Pour a dollop
Water to.

Butter, butter,
From just one cow;
Pour a dollop
Of water now.

6-4 BAKING COOKIES

Wäa well scheene Kooke backe,	Who will nice cookies bake,	She who cookies wants to bake,
Dee mott habe säwen Sache:	She must have seven things:	Seven things she has to take:
Eia enn Schmolt,	Eggs and lard,	Eggs and lard,
(T)socka enn Solt,	Sugar and salt,	Sugar and salt,
Malkj enn Mäl;	Milk and flour;	Flour and milk,
Safran moakt dee Kooke jäl.	Saffron makes the cookies yellow.	Saffron, a yellow tint to make.

6-5 NEW YEAR'S COOKIES

NOTE: Mennonites traditionally make round, sweet fritters, filled with raisins, as a New Year's Day treat. They are called New Year's cookies or *Portseltje*.

Ekj Kjeem aun jerant	I came on running	I came running here
(Mie weare de Bekse jetrant).	(Me were the pants ripped).	(It was the best time of the year);
Ekj sach dän Schorsteen rooke—	I saw the chimney smoking—	I saw your chimney smoking—
Ekj wist woll waut jie mooke:	I knew well what you making:	I knew what you were making:
Jie mooke scheene Niejoasch Kooke!	You making nice New Year's cookies!	You were making New Year's cookies!

Jäw jie mie eene,	Give you me one,	If given one,
Dan bliew ekj stone;	Then stay I standing;	Then I'll stand grieving;
Jäw jie mie twee,	Give you me two,	If given two,
Dan fang ekj aun too gone;	Then start I on to go;	Then I'll begin my leaving;
Jäw jie mie dree, feea, fiew toojlikj,	Give you me three, four, five together,	But given three, four, five together,
Dan wensch ekj ju daut gaunsse Himmelrikj.	Then wish I you the whole heaven's realm.	I'll wish for you the sunniest New Year's weather.

6-6 Pockets Empty

Ekj kjeem fomm Boajch jerant,
De Bekse weare jetrant,
De Fuppe weare holl,
Ekj mujcht dee weare foll.

I came from the hill running,
The pants were ripped,
The pockets were empty,
I wish they were full.

I came a-running down
The hill that leads from town;
My pockets empty were—
I wish something were there.

6-7 Wishing

Ekj wensch, ekj wensch—
Ekj sie en kjliena Mensch;
Wan ekj woa jrata senne,
Woa ekj bäta wensche kjenne.

I wish, I wish—
I am a little person;
When I will bigger be,
Will I better wishing can.

I wish, I plan—
But I'm a little man;
When I will bigger be,
Then I will wish more fruitfully.

6-8 Hans Butter-Bread

Saj, saj wada,
Wada läje:
Hauns kjemt no Hus
Omm Bottabroot too froage.
Mutta wea nijch tus,
Foda wea nijch tus—
Piep! sajcht de Mus
Emm Fäatus.

Say, say again,
Again lie:
Hans comes to home
For butter-bread to ask.
Mother was not at home,
Father was not at home—
Peep! says the mouse
In the front porch.

Say, say, say it;
Once more tell it:
Hans comes back home
To ask for bread and butter.
Mother was not home,
Father was not home—
"Peep!" says the mouse,
"Come get some."

6-9 Urchin-Boy

Benjeltje, ke-penjeltje,
Jefst mie waut—
Dan best en Enjeltje;
Jefst mie nuscht—
Dan best en Jietskjniepa!

Little urchin, little smurchin,
[If you] give me something—
Then [you] are a little angel;
[If you] give me nothing—
Then [you] are a stingy-beetle!

Urchin-boy, you urchin-boy,
Give me things—
You are my pride and joy;
Give me naught—
Then you're a penny-pincher!

6-10 JUST FIVE CENTS

Mama, Papa, Aupel, Bäa—
Fief (T)sent jeff et häa.

Mamma, Papa, apple pear—
Five cents give it here.

Mamma, Papa, apple, pear—
Five cents with me share.

6-11 LOVE ME, LOVE ME NOT

Best mie goot,
Kjeep mie en Hoot;
Best mie doll,
Kjeep mie en Boll.

Are [you] me good?—
Buy me a hat;
Are [you] me angry?—
Buy me a bull.

If you me love,
Buy me a dove;
If you don't care,
Buy me a bear.

6-12 ONE, TWO, THREE, FOUR

Eent, twee, dree, feea—
Peeta jinkj no Beea,
Johaun jinkj no Schnaups,
Enn du best en Koddajalaups.

One, two, three, four—
Peter went for beer,
John went for liquor,
And you are a ragged sap.

One, two, three, four—
Peter went for beer,
Johnnie went for wine,
And you are a Raggedy-Ann.

6-13 HUNGER

Mie hungat,
Mie schlungat,
Mie schlackat de Buck.

Me hungers,
Me shlungers,
Me shakes the belly.

I'm hungry—
My tummy
Wants something that's yummy.

6-14 MANNERS

Eascht Mumm,
Dan Oom,
Dan Sän,
Dan Spieltän.

First aunt,
Then uncle,
Then son,
Then show-tooth.

First aunt,
Then uncle,
Then son,
Then son-of-a-gun.

6-15 Eating

Sie stell,
Frat Mell,
Frat wada,
Best de Foakjel sien Fada.

Be still,
Devour sweepings,
Devour again,
[You] are the piggy his cousin.

Be still,
Eat swill,
Keep gulping,
You're eating a pig's helping.

6-16 Mitch, Pitch, Pepper Mill

Mitsch, Pitsch, Päpa-mäl—
Diene Kjinja fräte fäl;
Aule Dach en Dola Broot—
Nemm daut Biel enn schlo see doot.

Mitch, pitch, pepper mill—
Your children devour much;
Every day a dollar bread—
Take the hatchet and strike them dead.

Mitch, pitch, pepper mill—
All your children eat their fill;
Every day a dollar's bread—
Take an axe and strike them dead.

6-17 Hans Slim-n-Trim

Hauns Ullarijch—
Kjieltje wull hee nijch,
Spakj kjräjch hee nijch,
Aulsoo bleef hee hungarijch.

Hans Ullarijch—
Noodles wanted he not,
Bacon got he not,
Therefore stayed he hungry.

Hans Slim-n-Trim
Noodles weren't for him,
Ham was too grim,
Therefore stayed he sleek and slim.

6-18 Michael, Pichael

Mejchel, prejchel, lot mie läwe;
Daut baste Foagel woa ekj die jäwe;
Daut Foagel woat die Hei jäwe;
Daut Hei woascht du de Koo jäwe;
Dee Koo woat die Malkj jäwe;
Dee Malkj woat die Schmaunt jäwe;
Dee Schmaunt woat die Botta jäwe;
Dee Botta woascht du nom Häakja
    brinje;
Dee Häakja woat die Schoo moake.

Michael, pichael, let me live;
The best bird will I you give;
The bird will me hay give;
The hay will you the cow give;
The cow will you milk give;
The milk will you cream give;
The cream will you butter give;
The butter will you to weaver bring;
The weaver will you shoes make.

Michael, pichael, let me live;
The best of birds to you I'll give;
The bird to you will give some hay
The hay can you give to the cow;
The cow to you will give some milk
The milk to you will give some
    cream;
The cream to you will give some
    butter;
The butter can you to shoester take;
The shoester for you can new shoes
    make.

6-19 Barefoot Goslings

Ruzhe, Petruzhe,
Waut ruschelt emm Stroo?
De Janstjes gone boaft
Enn ha kjeene Schoo.
De Schusta haft Leestje
Enn Lada feloare—
Nu senn siene Janstjes
De Feetjes fefroare.

Ruzhe, Petruzhe [Petruschtje—
    little Peter],
What rustles in the straw?
The little geese go barefoot
And have no shoes.
The shoester has little last
And leather lost—
Now are his little geese
The little feet frozen.

Ruzhe, Petruzhe,
What rustles the straw?
The goslings go barefoot—
Without shoes, I saw.
The shoester has mislaid
His last and his leather,
And now little bare feet
Are cold in cold weather.

6-20 Shoester, Shoester

Schusta, Schusta, schnurr—
Haft Lada fonne Koo;
Hee moakt mie niee Schoo—
Schusta, Schusta, schnurr.

Shoester, shoester, *schnurr*—
Has leather from a cow;
He makes me new shoes—
Shoester, shoester, *schnurr*.

Shoester, shoester, shoe—
Has leather from a cow
To make me new shoes now—
Shoester, shoester, shoe.

6-21 Sleep Later

Fomm Schusta no Hus,
Schlope kaust tus.

From the shoester to home,
Sleeping [you] can [do] at home.

From shoester let's run—
To sleep is no fun.

6-22 PETER AND PAUL

Peeta enn Peewel jinje hauwe:
Peewel hauft sikj emm Foot—
Peeta jinkj enn road sikj doot.

Peter and Paul went mowing:
Paul mowed self in the foot—
Peter went and cried self dead.

Peter and Paul both went a-mowing:
Paul cut himself in the toe—
It was Peter who hopped to and fro.

6-23 ISAAK, SPRISAAK

Iesaak, Spriesack,
Schlenkjafoot,
Schleit siene Brut
Emm Kjalla doot.

Isaak, chaff-sack,
Shaky-foot,
Strikes his bride
In the cellar dead.

Isaak, sprisaak,
Twitchy-toe,
Strikes his fair bride
In the cellar a blow.

6-24 GEORGIE AND HORSIE

Jeat, schmeat,
Sett oppem Peat—
Ritt no Staut,
Koft siene Fru
En Bottafaut.

George, peorge,
Sat on the horse—
Rode to town,
Bought his woman
A butter churn.

Georgie, peorgie,
Sat on his horsie—
Rode into town
To buy his wife
A butter churn.

6-25 ANN, HITCH UP

NOTE: The "hill-and-dale" expression has its counterpart in the Mennonite place-name *Bergthal.*

Aunn, spaun aun;
'Trien, hool de Lien;
Mitsch, hol de Pitsch;
Soa, sat die nopp enn foa.

Ann, hitch on;
Kathrine, hold the lines;
Mary, fetch the whip;
Sarah, sit you on and drive.

Ann, hitch the team;
Kathrine, hold the reins;
Marie, you make three;
Sal, drive us o'er hill-and-dale.

6-26 John, Hitch Up

Johaun, spaun aun,
De Kaute feraun,
De Mies feropp—
Soo jeit et boajopp.

John, hitch on,
The cats before,
The mice in front—
So goes it uphill.

Now, John, hitch up
The cats with a will
And mice before them
For going uphill.

6-27 Lambkin's Little Mare

Laumtje haud en Kobbeltje—
Dee wea noch junkj fonn joare;
Säd eenmol too siene Oole,
Dee kaun ekj uck lang foare.

Little lamb had a little mare—
She was still young of years;
[He] said once to his old one,
She can I also a long time drive.

Lambkin had a little mare—
She was still young and thriving;
He said unto his good old wife,
She's good for years of driving.

6-28 Spring

De Kosebock sprinjt oppem Boajch;
De Janstjes rane wajch;
De Ul dee kjikjt fomm Boom erauf;
De Hoftje haft jelajcht.

The billy goat springs on the hill;
The little geese run away;
The owl he looks from the tree
    down;
The hawk has laid.

The billy goat springs on the hill;
The goslings run away;
The owl looks down from his
    treetop;
The hawk's laid an egg today.

6-29 SOMETHING NEW

Ekj weet waut niess—	I know something new—	To see it, you'll laugh—
De Koo haft en Kjiess.	The cow has a female calf.	The cow's a new calf.

6-30 FIDDLE AND FLUTE

Hauns mett de Fiddel,
Enn Jreet mett de Fleit;
Mutta, komm horjche
Woo scheen daut jeit.

Hans with the fiddle
And Greta with the flute;
Mother, come hear
How nice that goes.

Hans with the fiddle
And Kate with the flute;
Mother, come hear the
Tootle-to-toot.

6-31 BRUM, BRUM

NOTE: The *Brommtopp* was a homemade instrument of a cowhide drumhead stretched over the end of a wooden keg. A long horsehair whisk was fastened to the drumhead and when drawn between thumb and forefinger would produce a continuous droning sound. It was part of the New Year's Eve mumming tradition, common to some Mennonite people, where its accompaniment helped to announce a forecast of events for the coming year—see "The *Brommtopp* Song" in Chapter 9. In this nursery rhyme its approaching sound is more of an admonishment to a boy or girl to get at one's lessons.

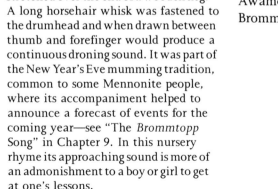

Lea, lea Lommtopp,
Morje kjemt de Brommtopp,
Äwamorje kjemt hee wada—
Bromm, bromm, bromm.

Learn, learn, boat-crock,
Tomorrow comes the *Brommtopp*,
Over tomorrow comes he again—
Brum, brum, brum.

Learn, learn, lum-dumb,
Tomorrow comes the brum-drum,
The day after will again come—
Brum, brum, brum.

SEVEN

Nursery Games

7-1 Butt the Head

Fia moake, Kjieltje koake—
Brat Schniedasch, komt äte;
Wan jie nijch woare äte kome,
Woa ekj mett ju Butskopp steete.

Fire make, noodles cook—
Board cutters, come eat;
If you will not eating come,
Will I with you butt-head bump.

Make the fire, cook the noodles—
Board sawyers, come for stew;
If you will not come and eat it,
I will then butt heads with you.

This rhyme is recited to a child on the parent's lap when they are face to face. The first three lines are simply there to work up to the climax of the last line, at which time the child and parent affectionately butt their foreheads together.

7-2 Little Rooster

Kjenntje, Multje,
Oogtje, Brontje,
Back enn Näs:
Schiep, schiep, mien Hontje.

Little chin, little mouth,
Little eye, little brow,
Cheek and nose:
Cheep, cheep, my little rooster.

Wee chin, wee mouth,
Wee eye, wee brow,
Cheek and nose:
Cheep, cheep, my rooster now.

As the baby is held on the mother's knee, facing her, the mother touches each of the facial features in turn as the verse is said and ends by gently pulling the hair above the child's forehead, its "rooster's comb."

61

7-3 Crow-a-Rie

Kjrei-a-rie,
De Hon ess doot—
Reat nijch meea
Mett een Foot.

Crow-a-rie,
The rooster is dead—
Stirs not more
With one foot.

Crow-a-rie,
The rooster's dead—
Stirs no wattle
Upon his head.

The child's foot is affectionately moved in a circle—or its wattle-chin is twitched.

7-4 Pinch-William

Wellem, kjnell'm,
Jriep'm, kjniep'm,
Kjnell'm wada,
Biet'm, schmiet'm.

William, punch'm [punch him],
Grip'm, pinch'm,
Punch'm again,
Bite'm, throw'm.

William, pinch'm,
Crunch'm, punch'm,
Fight'm, bite'm,
Boss'm, toss'm.

A child on the knee is teasingly pinched, seized, punched, bitten, and tossed.

7-5 Shuckle, Shuckle

Schockel, Schockel, scheia—
Oostre, ät wie Eia;
Pinjste, ät wie wittet Broot;
Stoaw' wie nijch,
Dan woa wie groot.

Swing, swing, *scheia*—
Easter, eat we eggs;
Pinkster, eat we white bread;
Die we not,
Then become we big.

Shuckle, shuckle, shia—
We'll eat eggs at Easter;
At Whitsuntide we'll eat white
  bread;
If we don't die,
Then we'll get by.

This is a rhyme to be said as a baby is rocked, either in a parent's arms or in a cradle. "Pinkster" is an English term still used in some parts of America to designate Pentecost or Whitsunday. Note the term's use in pinkster—or pinxter—flower. Cf. Dutch *Pinksteren*.

7-6 BILLY-GOAT, JUMP

Sprinj, Bockje, sprinj,	Spring, little billy goat, spring,	Jump, billy boat, jump,
Enn daut kole Goatje;	In the empty garden;	In the empty garden:
Kjemt de oola (T)sejona-maun	Comes the old gypsy man	Comes the wandering gypsy man
Enn ritt die aun daut Boatje.	And pulls you on the little beard.	And pulls your beard, beg your pardon.

The child is bounced on the parent's knee while the rhyme is said. As the last line is said, the parent chucks the child under its chin.

7-7 TRUCK, TRUCK, TREGGIE

Troch, Troch, treitje,	Trough, trough, *treitje*,	Truck, truck, treggie,
De Krauntje lajcht en Eitje;	The little crane lays a little egg;	The crane has laid an eggie;
De Kota wull daut no doone—	The tomcat wants that [likewise] to do—	The tomcat wants to do it too
Dee läd en groota Kjreihon!	He lays a great crow-rooster!	But lays a crowing rooster!

Dee Kjreihon flooch	The crow-rooster flew	The rooster flies
Däm Maun emm Boat;	The man in the beard;	Into your beard;
Dee maun kaun daut nijch liede,	The man could that not stand	But you—you cannot take it:
Enn schmiet am äwre Wiede.	And threw him over the willows.	Stick out your chin and shake it.

The child is bounced on the knee in time with the galloping rhythm of the first stanza. This is one of the most nonsensical of Mennonite rhymes, and there is a sudden stop in actions with the surprise ending of "rooster!"—one of the versions has *Krauphon*, a word of uncertain meaning. The actions now focus on the baby's chin, which is chucked, lifted up, and gently shaken. In the original *Plautdietsch* version, there is the action of nipping off the chin between thumb and forefinger and throwing "it" away.

7-8 Hop, Hop, Hop

Hupps, hupps, hupps, hupps, seedatje,	Hop, hop, hop, hop, *seedatje*,	Hop, hop, hop, hop, hop away,
Bäbe felt fomm Feedatje—	Baby falls from the little hayload—	Baby falls from the load of hay—
Kaum de Boll enn stad ar dol;	Comes the bull and bumps her down;	Comes the cow and bumps her down;
Kaum de Bock enn holp ar opp,	Comes the billy goat and helps her up,	Comes the buck and helps her up
Drooch ar enn daut witte Hustje.	Carries her into the little white house.	And carries her into the little white house.
Doa schlachte see Schwien;	There slaughter they swine;	There butchered are swine;
Doa drinkje see Wien;	There drink they wine;	There drunk is wine;
Doa daunst de Mus;	There dances the mouse;	There dances the mouse;
Doa fiddelt de Lus;	There fiddles the louse;	There fiddles the louse;
Doa flijcht de Kuckuck	There flies the cuckoo	There flies the cuckoo
Ut däm Fensta rut.	Out the window outside.	Out through the window.

The baby is bounced on its parent's knee during the first line of the rhyme. For the second line the parent spreads the knees so that the baby, while still being supported securely with its arms, falls through. This was nicely done in the days when mothers wore long full skirts. The child is helped up with reference to the billy goat and then rocked in rhythm to the remaining lines. Often just the first two lines of the rhyme were said, and these were repeated over and over.

7-9 The Road to Grandma's

Hupptje, Mauntje, riede,	Hoppy, little man, ride,	Hopalong, little man, ride away,
No de groote Wiede	To the great willows,	To the willows so big and gray,
Wua de groota Witt-boom steit,	Where the great white tree stands,	Where the great white birch tree stands,
Wua de Wajch no Groossmau jeit,	Where the way to Grandma goes.	Where the road to Grandma ends.

The child is bounced on the knee, or swung on the foot while riding "horsey," to the rhythm of the words.

7-10 LOPE, HORSEY, LOPE

Hupps, Kunta, riede
No de jäle Wiede;
Mette oole jriese Koo,
Foa wie no de Mäl opptoo.

De Mala saul daut mole—
Dee molt daut fäl too groff;
Daut Wief saul daut woll kjnäde—
Felt selfst mette Näs emm Troch.

Hop, gelding, ride,
To the yellow willows;
With the old gray cow,
Drive we to the mill towards.

The miller shall that mill—
He mills that much too coarse;
The wife shall that no doubt
   knead—
Falls self with her nose in the
   trough.

Lope, horsey, lope,
To the yellow willow;
With the old gray brindle cow,
We'll gallop to the mill-o.

The miller shall start milling
The wheat for good coarse bread;
His wife shall knead the bread
   dough—
Falls—swoosh!—on her nose
   instead.

This is another little game in which a youngster is bounced on the parent's knee. This is done during the saying of the first stanza, which has the rhythm of a horse's gallop. The child is bounced up and down while the parent holds the baby's hands in hers. The rhythm changes in the second stanza. Here the parent swings the child's hands in little circles to demonstrate the turning of the windmill sails or of the millstones. As the miller's wife kneads the dough, the parent moves the child's hands up and down, then bumps its head down with the final line of the stanza. NOTE: In Russia, the housewives usually kneaded their dough in a little wooden trough.

7-11 HOOT-RE-POOT

Haj, soo ritt dee Harschoft
Mett de blanke Pead;
Haj, soo ritt dee Koch
Mettem schmurtsja Rock;
Haj, soo ritt dee Ackamaun
Mett sien peatje hinjaraun,
Daut sajcht emma:
"Hutt-re-putt, hutt-re-putt, hutt-re-
   putt."

Heigh, so rides the gentry
With the shiny horses;
Heigh, so rides the cook
With the greasy coat;
Heigh, so rides the acre-man
With his little horse following,
That says always:
"Hoot-re-poot, hoot-re-poot, hoot-
   re-poot."

Heigh, so rides the gentry
With its shiny steeds;
Heigh, so rides the cook
With his greasy coat;
Heigh, so rides the farmer
With his pony following,
That always says:
"Hoot-re-poot, hoot-re-poot, hoot-
   re-poot."

This is a rhyme to be recited to a child as it rides "horsey" on a parent's foot. The foot may be swung high or low, slowly or vigorously, to accompany the various rides which are described.

7-12 HULL-LULL-LULL-LOO

Dume, schedde Plume;	Thumb, pour plums;	Thumb, shake down plums;
Du lass opp;	You, gather up;	You, gather up,
Du frat opp;	You, devour up;	You, eat them up,
Du saj, "Holl-loll-loll-loll";	You, say, "Hull-lull-lull-lull";	You, say, "Hull-lull-lull-loo";
Ekj woa Muttatje saje.	I will little Mother tell.	And I'll tell Mother on you.

This is said as the parent points to the five fingers on a child's hand, starting with the thumb. There is one line for each finger.

7-13 FINGER COUNTING

Kjliena Finja,	Little finger,	Little finger,
Golt Rinja,	Gold ringer,	Gold ringer,
Lank Hauls,	Long neck,	Long neck,
Botta Lekja,	Butter licker,	Butter licker,
Lustje Kjnekja.	Louse squasher.	Louse knocker.

This rhyme describes each finger on the child's hand. The child is taught to point to each finger in turn, starting with the little finger, as the rhyme is said. The last one, the thumb, is associated with the louse, for the thumb nail was good for squashing lice with a cracking sound.

7-14 ONE TO FIVE

Ekj enn du enn dee—	I and you and he—	You and I and he—
Daut senn dree;	That is three;	That makes three;
Jana enn sien Wief—	That one and his wife—	That one and his wife—
Daut senn fiew.	That is five.	That makes five.

This is a game to teach a child to count. The parent counts fingers on the baby's hand, starting with the little finger. She counts off the first three—"That makes three." Then she points to the thumb—"Jana," that is, the far one—and to the index finger that is paired with it. This couple—man and wife—along with the others, makes five in all.

7-15 ONE, TWO, THREE

Eent, twee, dree,
Botta oppem Brie,
Solt oppem Spakj—
Du best wajch.

One, two, three,
Butter on the porridge,
Salt on the bacon—
You are gone.

One, two, three,
Butter spread with glee,
Salt on the ham—
Down I cram.

There are actions for each line. One counts fingers for the first line, pretends to spread butter next, shakes salt vigorously on imaginary food, then gulps it down.

7-16 THE FLEA

Doa kome twee jegone,
See näme eenem jefange,
See näme am no Wribbel-wrips
Fonn Wribbel-wrips no Noagel-spets,
Enn doa woat hee doot jemoakt.

There come two walking,
They take one prisoner,
They take him to rubbing-[session],
From rubbing-[session] to nail-tip,
And there will he dead be made.

There come now two a-walking,
They take a third as prisoner,
They give him a good rubbing-out,
From rubbing-out to pressing flat,
And so is he made dead.

The two who come a-walking are finger and thumb moving along as a pair of legs. They catch an imaginary flea, and it is rubbed between the thumb and forefinger. Then it is pinched flat between the two thumb-nail tips. The action accompanies the rhyme to show how a flea is killed.

7-17 STIR THE PORRIDGE

Rea, rea, Jrettje;
Rea, rea, Jrettje—
Jeff däm waut,
Jeff däm waut,
Jeff däm waut,
Jeff däm waut;
Disem, riet de Kopp auf,
Enn schmiet am wajch.

Stir, stir, porridge;
Stir, stir, porridge—
Give him some,
Give him some,
Give him some,
Give him some;
This one, tear the head off,
And throw it away.

Stir and stir the porridge;
Stir and stir the porridge—
Give him some,
Give him some,
Give him some,
Give him some;
This one, off with his head,
And throw it away.

The parent takes the child's hands and teaches it the actions as the rhyme is said. With the first two lines, the child uses the index finger to inscribe circles on the palm of the other hand. As the next four lines are said, the child uses the same index finger to point to each of the fingers in turn on the other hand. With the final two lines, it pretends to tear off the remaining thumb and throw it away.

7-18 BAKING COOKIES

Backe, backe, Kooke;
Mältje ess emm Sackje;
Eitje ess emm Korwe;
Kuckuck ess jestorwe.
Wua well wie am seekje!—
Hinjre Schultse Ooke.
Schoaw auf, schoaw auf.

Bake, bake, little cookie;
Little flour is in the little sack;
Little egg is in the little basket;
Cuckoo is died.
Where will we him seek?—
Behind Schultz's eaves.
Shove off, shove off.

Baking, baking, cookies;
Flour is in the sack;
Eggs are in the basket;
The cuckoo bird has died.
Where will we now seek him?—
Under the Schultzes' eaves.
Dust off, dust off.

There are actions for the child to do as the words are said. For "baking cookies," it pats one hand on the other as though it were shaping or moulding them; for the second line, it dips flour out of a sack; for the third line, it forms a basket with its little hands; for the fourth line, it presses the palms of the hands together in a horizontal position. In seeking the lost cuckoo, the child holds out its hands questioningly, then points to imaginary eaves. For the last line, the child dusts imaginary flour off the front of its shirt or blouse, for the cookie baking is done.

7-19 WE ARE LITTLE BISCUITS

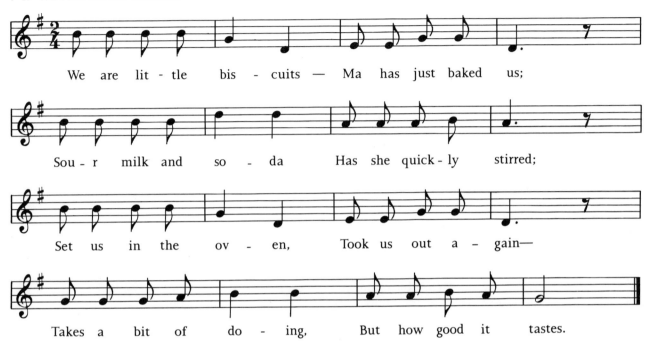

We are lit - tle bis - cuits — Ma has just baked us;

Sou - r milk and so - da Has she quick - ly stirred;

Set us in the ov - en, Took us out a - gain—

Takes a bit of do - ing, But how good it tastes.

NOTE: This melody is taken from an old German hymn, "Kleine Schnitter," by Karl Röhl and J. H. Weber. This hymn can be found in E. O. Margaret and Geo. J. Meyer, *Die Kleine Palme* (Chicago: Meyer and Brother, 1895). Even the first line of the rhyme is a parody of the hymn's first line: "Wir sind kleine Schnitter"—We are humble harvesters [literally cutters]. The *Plautdietsch* word for biscuits—*Schnetje*—has a similar derivation as "Schnitter" since the biscuits were not customarily round but *cut* into rectangles from the rolled-out dough.

Wie senn kjliene Schnetje—
Ma haft ons jebackt;
Sure Malkj enn Sooda
Haft see toop jereat;
Sat ons enn dän Owa,
Nemt ons wada rut—
Kost en bestje Oabeit,
Oba schmakjt uck goot.

We are little biscuits—
Ma has us baked;
Sour milk and soda
Has she together stirred;
Set us in the oven,
Took us again out—
Cost a bit work,
But tastes also good.

We are little biscuits—
Ma has just baked us;
Sour milk and soda
Has she quickly stirred;
Set us in the oven,
Took us out again—
Takes a bit of doing,
But how good it tastes.

There are motions to go with each line:
1. 1 — point to oneself.
1. 2 — show sour milk and soda.
1. 3 — stir in a bowl.
1. 4 — pretend to set pan into an oven.
1. 5 — take pan out.
11. 6–7 — act as if biscuits taste good and smack lips.

EIGHT

Children's Games

8-1 HEY, YOU MERRY ONE

Haj, du lostijch,
Ekj enn Hauns,
Wie senn one Sorje.

Hey, you merry [one],
I and Hans,
We are without sorrow.

We are merry,
Hans and I,
We, without real sorrow.

This is not a game per se but an expression of merriment given by children when they are about to play.

8-2 YOU AND I

Ekj enn du,
Kjeepe eene bunte schwoate Koo—
Waut dee Koo frat, weetst du.

I and you,
Buy a colorful black cow—
What the cow eats, know you.

You and I
A brindled cow of black and white
    will buy—
What it eats, know you, not I.

This is not a game in itself but a rhyme to say while pointing to players in turn—one to a stressed word—to determine who will be "it."

8-3 OAK AND BOAK

Äkje, bäkje, Boakjeholt
De Lied dee saje ekj sie stolt,
De Lied dee saje ekj sie domm—
Äkje, bäkje, Boakjeboom.

Oaks, boaks, birch-wood—
The people they say I am proud,
The people they say I am crazy—
Oaks, boaks, birch tree.

Oak and boak and birch-tree wood—
The people say that I am proud,
The people say that I am mad—
Oak and boak and birch-tree wood.

This is another rhyme to be recited in determining who will be "it" for a game.

8-4 BIFF, BOFF, OFF

Eene, meene, mekje (T)soagel—
Wäm wie kjrieje well wie joage,
Fonne Lien bat oppe Lada,
Dee soll heete Pomptje-mada—
Ädel, Bädel, biff, bauf, auf.

Eenie, meenie, *mekje* tail—
Whom we get will we chase,
From the line to up the ladder,
He shall [be] named little pump-
    mada—
Ädel, scoundrel, *biff, bauf,* off.

Eenie, meenie, donkey's tail—
Whom we get, him will we trail,
From the line up to the ladder,
He'll be mad and getting madder—
Adle, badle, biff, boff, off.

Again, this rhyme is repeated as children are counted off—one to a stressed word—to decide who will be "it" for a game. Note the several nonsense fillers.

8-5 Tag I

This rhyme is said in a taunting way at the person who is "it" in an ordinary game of tag.

Jriepa, Piepa,
Jript mie nijch;
Ess soo ful
Enn deit daut nijch.

Catcher, piper,
Catches me not;
Is so lazy
And does that not.

Tagger, bagger,
Tags me not;
Is so slow
And does it not.

8-6 Tag II

This is another taunting rhyme said by players to the person who is "it" in a game of tag.

Jriepa, Piepa,
Ekj sett oppe Huck;
Wan du kjemst,
Dan ran ekj fluck.

Catcher, piper,
I sit on the heels [squat];
When you come,
Then run I hastily.

Tagger, bagger,
I sit in the sun;
When you come,
Then away I run.

8-7 Old Blind Cow

—Blinje Koo, ekj leid die.
—Wua han?
—Nom Boare Staul.
—Boa bitt mie.
—Nemm en Stock enn wää die.

—Blind cow, I lead you.
—Where thither?
—To the bear barn.
—Bear bites me.
—Take a stick and defend you[rself].

—Old blind cow, I lead you.
—Where to?
—To the bear den.
—Bear bites me.
—Take a stick and watch out.

This is a Blindman's Buff. The blindfolded player is led by another player amid the others while the two of them repeat these statements in turn. At the last line the "Blindman" is let go so that he can begin to try to catch the others.

8-8 ALL BELOVED GOSLINGS

—Aule leewe Janstjes, komt no mie.
—Wie kjäne nijch.
—Wuaromm nijch?
—De Wulf ess doa.
—Waut deit dee doa?
—Lajcht Eia.
—Woo fäl?
—Feftian enn en Kjlienatje.
—Woont ess mient?
—Daut Goldna.
—Woont ess dient?
—Daut Selwana.
—Woont ess dee Wolf sient?
—Daut Fula.
—Aule leewe Janstjes, komt no mie.

—All beloved little geese, come to me.
—We cannot.
—Why not?
—The wolf is there.
—What does he there?
—Lays eggs.
—How many?
—Fifteen and a little, little one.
—Which is mine?
—The gold one.
—Which is yours?
—The silver one.
—Which is the wolf his?
—The rotten one.
—All beloved little geese, come to me.

—All beloved goslings, come to me.
—We cannot come.
—Why not?
—The wolf is there.
—What does he do?
—Lays eggs.
—How many?
—Fifteen and a little one.
—Which is mine?
—The gold one.
—Which is yours?
—The silver one.
—Which is the wolf's egg?
—The rotten one.
—All beloved goslings, come to me.

This is a question-and-answer game. The "Mother Goose" stands at one line, while all but one of the other children, the "goslings," stand at another line, facing her. The remaining child, the "wolf," stands along one of the sidelines. Then begins the conversation between Mother Goose and her goslings. When she comes to the last line, the goslings must leave their line of safety and run to her. The wolf meanwhile tries to tag as many as he can before they reach her line of safety.

Then the Mother Goose goes to the other line, and the game goes on again, continuing in this fashion until the wolf has caught all the goslings. The last one caught becomes the new Mother Goose, while the first one tagged has to be the new wolf as the game begins anew.

8-9 WANDERER'S SONG

Komm, wie welle waundre,
Fonn eene Staut no de aundre,
Bat wie nijch meea wieda kjäne:
Liestje, Liestje, drei die omm.

Come, we want to wander,
From one town to the other,
Till we not more farther can:
Little Liesa, little Liesa, turn you
   around.

Come, we want to wander,
From town to town meander,
Till we can no farther go:
Liesa, Liesa, turn around.

Two children walk side by side, holding each other's hands behind their backs—left hand with left hand, right with right—while repeating this stanza. When they come to the last line, they turn sharply halfway around, each to the outside, without letting go each other's hands. They then walk in the opposite direction as they say the stanza again. The game is repeated indefinitely.

8-10 ROUND AND ROUND THE ROSY CROWN

Runde, runde, Roosekrauns,
Weppestauns,
Kjlinkjs dol,
Noch emol—
Aule kjliene Kjinja faule dol.

Round, round, roses-garland,
Pedal-stance,
Clink down,
Yet once more—
All little children fall down.

Round and round the rosy crown,
Curtsy then,
Squat down,
Once again—
All the little children tumble down.

This is a circle game, with children holding hands, moving in a ring as if around a rosebush, and doing the described actions.

8-11 THE BRIDGE HAS NOW BEEN BROKEN

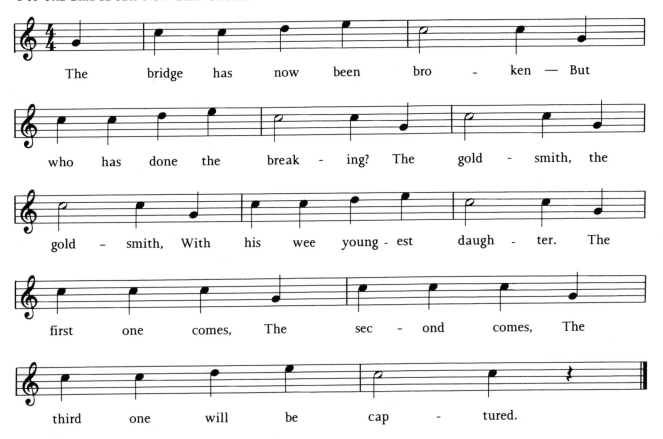

The bridge has now been bro - ken — But

who has done the break - ing? The gold - smith, the

gold - smith, With his wee young - est daugh - ter. The

first one comes, The sec - ond comes, The

third one will be cap - tured.

De Brigj dee ess jebroake—
Wää haft dee dan jebroake?
De Goltschmett, de Goltschmett,
Mett siene jinjste Dochta.
De easchte kjemt,
De tweede kjemt,
De dredde woat jefange.

The bridge it is broken—
Who has it then broken?
The goldsmith, the goldsmith,
With his youngest daughter.
The first one comes,
The second comes,
The third one will be captured.

The bridge has now been broken—
But who has done the breaking?
The goldsmith, the goldsmith,
With his wee youngest daughter.
The first one comes,
The second comes,
The third one will be captured.

This is a singing game for little children, preschoolers, similar to "London Bridge Is Falling Down." Here, however, the two children forming an arch hold their hands linked together at waist level. One child holds her hands palm upwards and the other child palm downwards so that their curled fingers hook into each other's.

The ring of children who pass under the arch do not step forward under the arch. Instead, they have linked hands with each other to form a continuous ring, each child facing into the center of the circle. This continuous ring now passes sideways under the arch. Each child in turn has to duck down to get underneath but does not let go her handgrasp with the others. All the children sing the song as the game is played, and the children keep ducking under the arch.

When the fifth line is sung—"The first one comes"—the two children forming the arch loop their arms around the child passing underneath, but then let her go. The same thing is done as the next line is sung and the "second" child passes underneath. But the "third" child is captured as the final line is sung. This child stands aside and is out of the game, which continues over and over until only two children are left in the ring to pass under the arch. These two children will form the arch for the next round of the game.

NINE

Songs

9-1 SINGING, HI!

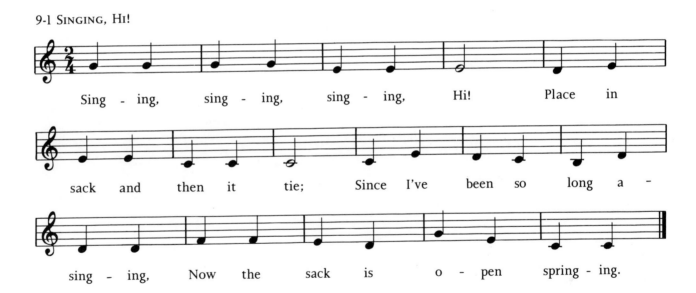

Sing - ing, sing - ing, sing - ing, Hi! Place in sack and then it tie; Since I've been so long a - sing - ing, Now the sack is o - pen spring - ing.

Sinj'm [sinj too am], sinj'm, sinj'm, soo,
Stopp emm Sack enn binj'm [binj am] too;
Haud ekj nijch soo lang jesunge,
Wea dee Sack nijch op jesprunge.

Sing it [him], sing it, sing it, so,
Stick into the sack and tie it [him] to;
Had I not so long sung,
Were the sack not open sprung.

Singing, singing, singing, Hi!
Place in sack and then it tie;
Since I've been so long a-singing,
Now the sack is open springing.

9-2 Come If You Will

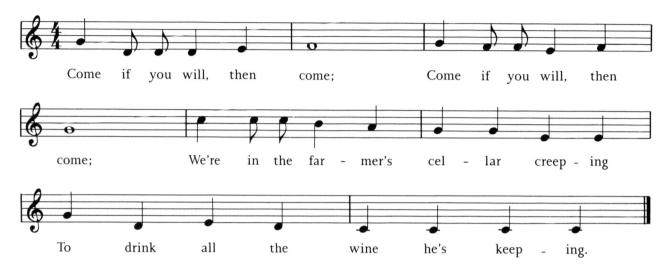

Come if you will, then come; Come if you will, then
come; We're in the far - mer's cel - lar creep - ing
To drink all the wine he's keep - ing.

Komm wan du west, dan komm;	Come if you want, then come;	Come if you will, then come;
Komm wan du west, dan komm;	Come if you want, then come;	Come if you will, then come;
Well wie däm Bua emm Kjalla krupe,	Will we the farmer in the cellar creep	We're in the farmer's cellar creeping
Enn am aule Wien ut supe.	And him all the wine out guzzle.	To drink all the wine he's keeping.

9-3 Lot Is Dead

Lot is dead, Lot is dead, Lie - sa's on her death - bed; That is good, that is good, We will much in - her - it. One will now get some but - tered bread, An - oth -er'll get a chick - en head; That is good, that is good, We will much in - her - it.

Lott ess doot, Lott ess doot, Liestje lijcht opp stoawe; Daut ess goot, daut ess goot, Woa wie uck waut oawe.	Lot is dead, Lot is dead, Little Liesa lies on dying; That is good, that is good, Will we also something inherit.	Lot is dead, Lot is dead, Liesa's on her death-bed; That is good, that is good, We will much inherit.
Eene oaft en Steck Botta-broot, Dee aundre oaft en Heena-foot; Daut ess goot, daut ess goot, Woa wie uck waut oawe.	One inherits a piece butter-bread, The other inherits a chicken foot; That is good, that is good, Will we also something inherit.	One will now get some buttered bread, Another'll get a chicken head; That is good, that is good, We will much inherit.

9-4 THE *BRUMMELS* SONG

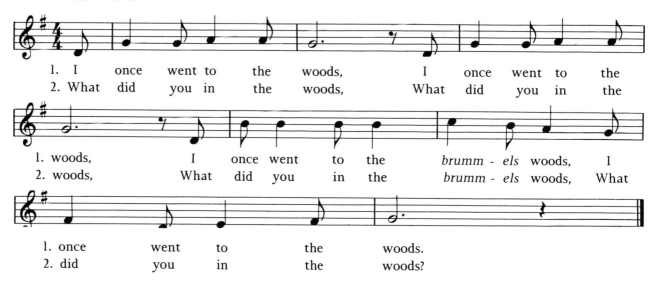

1. I once went to the woods,
   I once went to the
2. What did you in the woods,
   What did you in the

1. woods,
   I once went to the *brumm - els* woods, I
2. woods,
   What did you in the *brumm - els* woods, What

1. once went to the woods.
2. did you in the woods?

1. Ekj jinkj emol nom Woolt,
   Ekj jinkj emol nom Woolt,
   Ekj jinkj emol nom brummels
      Woolt,
   Ekj jinkj emol nom Woolt.

2. Waut deedst du enn dän Woolt,
   Waut deedst du enn dän Woolt,
   Waut deedst du enn dän
      brummels Woolt,
   Waut deedst du enn dän Woolt?

3. Ekj socht mie doa woll Struck.
4. Waut deedst du mett daut
      Struck?
5. Ekj brennd mie daut too Ausch.
6. Waut deedst du mett dee Ausch?
7. Ekj mook mie dan woll Loog.
8. Waut deedst du mett dee Loog?
9. Ekj koakt mie dan mien Hamd.
10. Waut funkst du enn daut Hamd?

1. I went once to the woods,
   I went once to the woods,
   I went once to the *brummels*
      woods,
   I went once to the woods.

2. What did you in the woods,
   What did you in the woods,
   What did you in the *brummels*
      woods,
   What did you in the woods?

3. I sought me there indeed brush.
4. What did you with the brush?
5. I burned me that to ash.
6. What did you with the ash?
7. I made me then indeed lye.
8. What did you with the lye?
9. I boiled me then my shirt.
10. What found you in the shirt?

1. I once went to the woods,
   I once went to the woods,
   I once went to the *brummels*
      woods,
   I once went to the woods.

2. What did you in the woods,
   What did you in the woods,
   What did you in the *brummels*
      woods,
   What did you in the woods?

3. I sought me there some brush.
4. What did you with the brush?
5. I burned it down to ash.
6. What did you with the ash?
7. I made me then some lye.
8. What did you with the lye?
9. I boiled and washed my shirt.
10. What found you in the shirt?

11. Ekj funk doa woll ne Lus.	11. I found there indeed a louse.	11. I found me there a louse.
12. Waut deedst du mett dee Lus?	12. What did you with the louse?	12. What did you with the louse?
13. Ekj ladat dee woll auf.	13. I leathered him indeed off.	13. I skinned its leather off.
14. Waut deedst du mett daut Lada?	14. What did you with the leather?	14. What did you with the leather?
15. Ekj mook mie dan woll Schoo.	15. I made me then indeed shoes.	15. I made me then some shoes.
16. Wua jinkjst du dan woll han?	16. Where went you then indeed hither?	16. Where did you walk with them?
17. Ekj jinkj dan woll no Kjoakj.	17. I went then indeed to church.	17. I then walked out to church.
18. Waut säde dan de Lied?	18. What said then the people?	18. What did the folks then say?
19. Dee säde ekj wea domm!	19. They said I was crazy!	19. They said that I was nuts!

In the stanzas of this question-and-answer song, each line is repeated four times with the word *brummels* always added as the second-last word in the third line. *Brummels* means "grumbles" but is here used as a nonsense word.

9-5 The *Brommtopp* Song

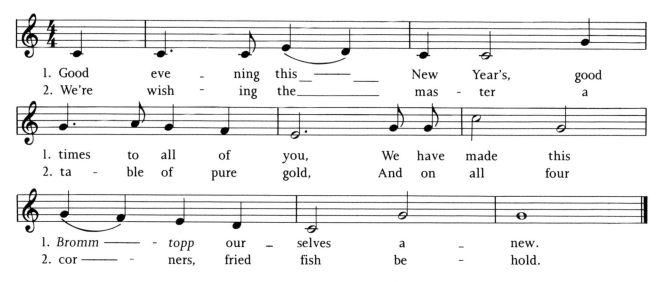

1. Good eve - ning this_____ New Year's, good
2. We're wish - ing the_____ mas - ter a

1. times to all of you, We have made this
2. ta - ble of pure gold, And on all this four

1. *Bromm*——-*topp* our _ selves a _ new.
2. cor——-ners, fried fish be - hold.

NOTE: In most folksongs there may be several versions, both in melody and words, of a single song. "The *Brommtopp* Song" is no exception. Over the years different performers have varied the melody line and also adapted the words and/or added or deleted stanzas to make the meaning appropriate to the family being addressed.

The singers, as attested in the explanation following "Brum, Brum" in the "Nursery Rhymes" chapter, were traditional mummers—here young people in some Mennonite communities who would go from door to door on New Year's Eve, dressed in masquerade costume, and carrying their *Brommtopp* previously described. In presenting their well wishes in song, as well as a few good-natured admonishments, to members of each household, they hoped with their high-spirited fun to gain a few coins for their efforts—but would be satisfied enough with a gift of some

1. En scheena gooda Owent enn eene schaftje Tiet,
Dän Brommtopp ha wie ons selfst jemoakt.

2. Wie wensche däm Har en goldna Desch,
Opp aule feea Akje en jebrodna Fesch.

3. Enne Medd, enne Medd, eene Kaun mett Wien,
Doamett ons Har kaun lostijch senne.

4. Wie wensche de Fru ne goldne Kroon,
Opp en aundret Joa en schmock junga Sän.

1. A nice good evening and a happy time,
The *Brommtopp* have we ourselves made.

2. We wish the master a golden table,
On all four corners a fried fish.

3. In the middle, in the middle, a can with wine,
There with our master can jolly be.

4. We wish the wife a golden crown,
On the coming [different] year a nice young son.

1. Good evening this New Year's, good times to all of you,
We have made this *Bromm-topp* ourselves anew.

2. We're wishing the master a table of pure gold,
And on all four corners, fried fish behold.

3. And there in the middle a jug of wine for thee,
So that our master now will jolly be.

4. We're wishing the mistress a shiny golden crown,
In the coming year a well-mannered son.

Mennonite New Year's fritters or *Portseltje*. Further explanation, alluded to elsewhere, can be found in J. G. Toews, "Traditional Mennonite Pastimes," in Julius G. Toews and Lawrence Klippenstein, eds., *Manitoba Mennonite Memories*, 1974.

5. Wie wensche de Dochta eene
selwane Kaun
Opp en aundret Joa en schmock
junga Maun.

6. Wie wensche daut Mäakje en
lijcht rooda Rock,
Opp en aundret Joa mettem
Bassem-stock.

7. Wie wensche de Kjäakjsche eene
heltene Kaun,
Opp en aundret Joa en
pucklijcha Maun.

8. Wie wensche däm Sän en
jesodeltet Peat,
En Poa Pistoole enn en blanket
Schweat.

9. Wie wensche däm Kjnacht eene
Schrop enn Scheea,
Daut hee kaun putse däm Har
sien Peat.

10. Wie wensche däm Schwienhoad
eene Knutt enne Haunt,
Daut hee kaun driewe de Kujels
emm Launt.

11. Wie heare däm Bua mette
Schlätels kjlinjre,
Enn wie dochte hee wudd ons en
Golt-steck brinje.

5. We wish the daughter a silver
can,
On the coming year a nice young
man.

6. We wish the small girl a light red
skirt,
On the coming year [a licking]
with the broomstick.

7. We wish the kitchen-maid a
wooden can,
On the coming year a
hunchbacked man.

8. We wish the son a saddled horse,
A pair of pistols and a shiny
sword.

9. We wish the hired man a
currycomb and shears,
That he can groom the master
his horse.

10. We wish the swineherd a cudgel
in the hand,
That he can drive the boars in
the land.

11. We hear the farmer with keys
ringing,
And we thought he would us a
gold-piece bring.

5. We're wishing the daughter a
pretty silver can,
In the coming year a young
handsome man.

6. We're wishing the young girl a
red skirt and a comb,
In the coming year a cuff with
the broom.

7. We're wishing the housemaid a
sturdy wooden can,
In the coming year an old
hunchbacked man.

8. We're wishing the young son the
nicest saddled horse,
And a pair of pistols and shiny
sword.

9. We're wishing the hired man a
shears and currycomb,
So that for the master his horse
can groom.

10. We're wishing the swineherd a
cudgel for his hand,
So that he can drive the pigs
through the land.

11. We're hearing the farmer—his
keys how they do ring.
And we thought he would us a
gold-piece bring.

In the stanzas, the fourth syllable in the first line and the fifth syllable in the second line both receive a slurred note. It should be pointed out that in the earlier *Plautdietsch* version the metric pattern is not completely regular so that there the words need a Procrustes-like adjustment to the music.

TEN

Riddles, Jokes, and Tongue-Twisters

10-1 RIDDLE I: HIGH HANGS HENDRIK

	AUNTWUAT		ANSWER		ANSWER
Hooch henjt Hendrikj;	*Klock*	High hangs Hendrik;	*clock*	On the wall—tick-tock;	*clock*
Biem Bad bullat et;	*Wäj*	By the bed, clatters it;	*cradle*	By the bed—click-clock;	*cradle*
Unjrem Owe—mie-au;	*Kaut*	Under the stove—meow;	*cat*	Under the stove—meow;	*cat*
Emm tus—hau;	*Hunt*	In the home—bow-wow;	*dog*	In the porch—bow-wow;	*dog*
Emm Staul—runt;	*Borm*	In the barn—round;	*well*	In the yard—creak-creak;	*well*
Bute—bunt.	*Stearens*	Outside—bright.	*stars*	(with pulley and bucket)	
				Up above—peek-peek.	*stars*

Each line refers to an object, which the listener tries to identify.

10-2 RIDDLE II: A GREAT BIRD

Doa flooch en Foagel stoakj	There flew a bird fast	There flew a bird so far
Äwrem lange Moakj.	Over the long market.	O'er seas to a bazaar.
Waut haud hee enn sien Kropp?—	What had he in his crop?—	What had it in its crop?—
Fief tonne Hopp,	Five tuns hops,	Five tuns of hops,
Fief tonne Beea,	Five tuns beer,	Five tuns of beer,
De Schnieda enn de Scheea,	The tailor and the shears,	The tailor and his shears,
De Miera mett de Kjall.	The mason with the trowel.	The blacksmith and his bellows.
Wäa ditt rot, ess Junkj-jesall.	Who this guesses, is young fellow.	Who guesses this are good young fellows.

AUNTWUAT: *Schepp*   ANSWER: *ship*   ANSWER: *ship*

84

10-3 RIDDLE III: JINGLE-MAN AND CLATTER-MAN

Kjlinja-maun enn Klaupa-maun
Jinje beid aum Boajch hinaun;
Klaupa-maun jinkj noch soo seea,
Enn Kjlinja-maun kjeem doch noch
    eea.

AUNTWUAT:
Kjlinja-maun—Pead mett Säle
Klaupa-maun—Woage

Jingle-man and clatter-man
Went both to the hill against;
Jingle-man went yet as fast,
And clatter-man came still yet
    sooner.

ANSWER:
jingle-man—horses and
    harness
clatter-man—wagon

Jingle-man and clatter-man
Both up the hill began;
Clatter-man went twice as fast,
But jingle-man still came in first.

ANSWER:
jingle-man—horses and their
    harness
clatter-man—wagon

The clattering wheels of the wagon—the "clatter-man"—go much faster in their turning than do the horses themselves along with their jingling harness—the "jingle-man." Yet the horses always stay ahead of the wagon and reach the destination first.

10-4 MEALTIME

Froag: Waut hast too Meddach?
Auntwuat: Nuscht mett *nä*, enn
    mett *jo* too jedakjt.

Question: What have [you] to
    dinner?
Answer: Nothing with *no*, and with
    yes covered.

Question: What do you have for
    dinner?
Answer: Nothing covered with *no*,
    and everything with *yes*.

No and *yes* are made concrete terms here. The image has to do with an older practice of placing cloth covers over food to keep it warm.

10-5 Greetings I

Gaust: Gooda-morje, one Sorje!
Weat: Scheen jesunt, oola Hunt?
Gaust: Haulw-wäaj, oole Sääj.

Guest: Good-morning, without sorrow!
Host: Good health, old dog?
Guest: Half-way, old sow.

Guest: Good-morrow, without sorrow!
Host: Not sick, old stick?
Guest: So-so, old crow.

When two old friends greet each other, the trick here is to be the first one to say the opening line of this set piece. The other then is obliged to say the second line, with the result that he is good-naturedly called an old sow, or old crow, in the final line.

10-6 Greetings II

Froag: Woo jeit et?
Auntwuat: Opp twee Been, auss en Gaunta.

Question: How goes it?
Answer: On two legs, like a gander.

Question: How are things going?
Answer: On two legs, like a gander.

There is a play on words here, centering on the word *jeit*. It can mean "walk" specifically—or "go" generally.

10-7 Your Fortune

Ekj saj die woa:
Oppem Kopp hast Hoa;
Ekj saj die ditt,
Ekj saj die daut,
P-s-s-t! diene Haunt ess naut.

I say you true:
On the head have hair;
I say you this,
I say you that,
P-s-s-t! your hand is wet.

I say with care:
Your head has hair;
The fortune you
Expect to get—
P-s-s-t! your hand is wet.

This joke is played between two boys. The first pretends to read the other's fortune by looking at the other's open palm, which he holds. With the last line, the palm-reader spits into the hand with the pronouncement that the other's hand is wet.

10-8 Beet Leaf

Grootet, roodet, breedet Beete-blaut.

Great, red, broad beet leaf.

Big, red, broad beet leaf.

The trilled *r*'s in *Plautdietsch* make this a more difficult tongue-twister in that language than in the English version.

10-9 WE WHITE WORKING WIVES

Wie witte Wiewa welle witte Winjle wausche,
Wan wie wiste wua woamet weekjet Wota wea;
Oba wan wie witte Wiewa wensche wudde,
Wudd woll woamet weekjet Wota woare.

We white wives want white diapers to wash,
If we knew where warm soft water was;
But if we white wives wish would
Would indeed warm soft water be.

We white working wives want to wash white woollens,
If we only wist where warm whirling water was;
But if we white working wives only would wish well,
Then would warm and whirling water well up.

10-10 THE TWO DIRK DYCKS

NOTE: Among early-day Mennonites, children were named after relatives, so that the same names cropped up again and again and there was always some trouble during conversations in distinguishing among like-named individuals. This tongue-twister, in part, is making fun of this situation.

Derkj Dycke Derkj drooch
Dän Derkj Dycke Derkj derjch
Däm dicke Duwe-drakj derjch;
Dan dankt dee Derkj Dycke Derkj
Dän Derkj Dycke Derkj
Daut dee Derkj Dycke Derkj
Dän Derkj Dycke Derkj derjch
Däm dicke Duwe-drakj derjch
drooch.

Dirk Dyck's Dirk carried
The [other] Dirk Dyck's Dirk through
The thick dove dirt through.
Then thanked the Dirk Dyck's Dirk
The [other] Dirk Dyck's Dirk
That the Dirk Dyck's Dirk
The [other] Dirk Dyck's Dirk through
The thick dove dirt through carried.

One Dirk Dyck's Dirk toted
Another Dirk Dyck's Dirk
Through the thick dove dirt.
Then the first Dirk Dyck's Dirk
Thanked the other Dirk Dyck's Dirk
That one Dirk Dyck's Dirk
Had been toted by
The other Dirk Dyck's Dirk
Through the thick dove dirt.

If there is still some confusion, remember that two older men, both named Dirk Dyck, each have a son named Dirk. It is the two sons who appear in this tongue-twister.

ELEVEN

Maxims About Marriage and Raising Children

11-1   Flekj opp' Loch,
       Die näm ekj noch;
       Knoppe fäarem Been,
       Du blifst auleen.

Patch on hole,
You take I still;
Knot before the leg,
You stay alone.

Patch-on-skirt—
Still marriageable;
Knot-before-the-knee—
Disparageable!

A young man would marry a girl with a patch on her skirt but not a girl who is too lazy to patch her dress but instead closes up the hole by tying the frayed ends of the cloth there into a knot.

11-2   Wan de leewa Gott well en Noa
       seene, dan lat Hee däm Maun de
       Fru stoawe.

When the loving God wants to see a fool, He lets a man's wife die.

11-3   Mutta doot:
       Foda blint,
       Kjant nijch meea
       Sien äjnet Kjint.

Mother dead:
Father blind,
Knows no more
His own child.

Mother—dead;
Father—blind,
Casts his children
From his mind.

A widower, once remarried, is so engrossed in his new wife that he forgets about the children of his first marriage.

NOTE: If a maxim is also a rhyme, then two translations are usually provided, as has been done for all previous items. Otherwise, the maxims and expressions in the following chapters receive a single translation, which conveys the meaning in everyday English (an equivalent saying may be included).

11-4   Waut de Maun mett däm Heirekj nenn brinje kaun, daut kaun de Fru mett däm Schaldook rut droage.

What the husband brings in with the hayrack, the wife carries out with her apron. (No matter how much money a husband makes, a wife can spend it in no time.)

11-5   Daut mach de Han weete wan de Hon nijch tus ess.

When the rooster's away, the hen wants a full accounting.

11-6   Kjinja froage mett (T)socka bestreit.

Children's questions are sprinkled with sugar. (There is a sweetness or naivete about the questions.)

11-7   Wan daut Mustje saut ess, ess daut Kuarntje betta.

When the little mouse is full, then is the kernel bitter. ("Mouse" refers affectionately to a child.)

11-8   Kjliene Kjinja, kjliene Sorje; groote Kjinja, groote Sorje.

Little children, little cares; bigger children, bigger cares.

11-9   Kjliene Kjinja drekje de Schoot; groote Kjinja drekje daut Hoat.

Little children press down on the lap; big children weigh much upon the heart.

11-10 De Aupel felt nijch wiet fomm Boom.

The apple doesn't fall far from the tree.

11-11 Soo Mutta, soo Kjint.

Like mother, like child.

11-12 Kjinja-mot enn Kjalwa-mot motte oole Lied weete.

Older people know what's best for calves and children (what portions or limits they should have).

11-13 Kjinja schlajcht opptrakje ess nijch blooss en Fäla; daut ess en grootet Febräakje.

Bringing up children badly is not just a failing—it's a great crime.

11-14 Waut Haunstje nijch leat, woat Hauns niemols leare.

What little Hans doesn't learn, big Hans will never learn.

11-15 Junkj jewant, oolt jedone.

Accustomed when young, done when old. (As the twig is bent, the tree shall grow.)

11-16   Läje haft korte Been.

Lying has short legs (it will get you nowhere).

11-17   Krakjtijchkjeit ess et haulwe Läwe; Kjinja, riemt dän Desch auf.

Tidiness is half of living; children, clean off the table.

11-18   Onnjeschekjte mott wajch!

Clumsiness (or incompetence) must go!

11-19   Wan de Heene kjreie enn de Mejales piepe, dän fält de Kopp auf too riete.

When hens crow and girls whistle, they both need to lose their heads.

11-20   Bat hia enn wieda nijch!

To here but no further!

11-21   Eizha, azha, Klostje, Täa Stäla!

Ah-hah, little Klaas, tar stealer! (This is said when a child is caught in the act of doing something it should not.)

11-22   En "muss" ess en Schwank;
Wäa nijch well, kjrijcht mettem Strank.

A "must" is a "have-to";   A duty is a command:
Who not wants, gets with a rope.   Or else a strap across the hand.

11-23   Wäa nijch heare well, mott feele.

Who won't listen, must feel the blow.

11-24   Daut ess Friedach fe däm dee nijch Priejel kjrijcht.

It's Friday for him who doesn't get a licking. (Meaning is uncertain: Friday may be a favored day because it is the last day of school for the week.)

11-25   Eent flooch oost,
Enn eent flooch wast,
Enn eent flooch äwa däm Kuckuck's Nast.

One flew east,
And one flew west,
And one flew over the cuckoo's nest.

This is about children leaving home and scattering far and wide. There is the possibility of one not settling down to family responsibilities—the European cuckoo lays its eggs in other birds' nests.

TWELVE

Maxims for Housewives

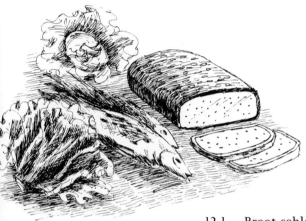

12-1 Broot schleit de Hunga doot.

Bread strikes hunger dead. (Bread is the staff of life.)

12-2 Fesch enn (T)selot
      Ess fe mie ne Tracktot.

Fish and lettuce
Is for me a treat.

Lettuce and fish—
For me what a dish!

12-3 Daut schmakjt nijch no am, uck
      nijch no ar.

This food tastes neither like him nor like her (neither fish nor fowl—does
      not taste one way or another).

12-4 Daut kost woll, oba daut schmakjt
      uck.

That costs much, but then it tastes good too. (The more you pay, the more
      it's worth.)

12-5 Wäa eenmol waut äwa lat, kaun
      tweemol Moltiet hoole.

He who makes a frugal meal can eat a second time.

12-6 Wäa nijch too Tiet toom äte kjemt,
      Mott äte waut am ess bestemmt.

Who not in time to eating comes,
Must eat what him is allotted.

Who doesn't come on time to eat,
Must eat what's left and that's no treat.

12-7 Fäl Jast
      Moakt en ladjet Nast.

Many a guest
Makes an empty nest.

The guests eat one out of house and home.

12-8 Wan aules aum Desch opp jejäte ess,
dan jeft et scheenet Wada.

When everything's been eaten from the table, then there'll be nice weather.

12-9 De Kjäakjsche enn de Kaut
Senn emma saut.

The cook and the cat
Are always fat.

12-10 Jedult enn goot äte—doamett kjemt
Maun aum wietste.

Forbearance and good eating—with these man will go farthest.

12-11 Jreen enn root
Sitt emma goot.

Green and red
Look always good.

Red and green—
Good to be seen.

12-12 Straum oppe Strot,
Enn schwiensch enne Kot.

Pretty on the street,
And swinish in the cottage.

Pretty up town,
At home dirty gown.

12-13 Fonn fäare—uj, uj!
Fonn hinja—fuj, fuj!

From in front—my, my!
From behind—fie, fie!

This is an admonition that things should be neat and clean throughout, and not only to outward appearance.

12-14 Kjleeda moake Lied,
Blooss daut ess nijch woa;
Selwa, Golt, enn Sied
Drajcht uck maunche Noa.

Clothes make people—
Only that is not true;
Silver, gold, and silk
Wears also many a fool.

Clothes now make the man—
But that is *not* true;
Silver, gold, and silk
Clothe fools and many too.

12-15 Wan see kjaft waut see nijch bruckt,
woat see boolt brucke waut see
nijch kjeepe kaun.

Who buys what she doesn't need will soon need what she can't buy.

12-16   Aule säwen Joa paust een Flekj.   Every seven years a patch will find use. (Waste not, want not. If a piece of cloth is not wasted but saved for a future patch, it will be sure to be needed before seven years are up.)

12-17   Langet Drot—
Fule Not.

Long thread—
Lazy seam.

Long stitch—
Poor patch.

12-18   Fäl' Henj
Moake schwinn en Enj.

Many a hand
Makes work soon end.

(Many hands make quick work.)

12-19   Oost, wast—
Tus ess et baste.

East, west—
Home is best.

THIRTEEN

Maxims for Farmers

13-1 Wan en Hon kjreit
Ea hee schlope jeit,
Dan wakjt hee opp
Wan et räajne deit.

When a rooster crows
Ere he to sleep goes
Then wakes he up
When it rain does.

When a cock crows
Ere to sleep he goes,
Then he'll arise
Under rainy skies.

13-2 Wan de Hon kjreit oppem Mest, dan endat daut Wada ooda blift auss et ess.

When the cock crows on his dunghill, then the weather will change or stay as it is.

13-3 Wan de Spreeje sinje, dan jeft et schlajchtet Wada.

When blackbirds sing, then bad weather's coming.

13-4 Wan de Wilw jule, dan jeft et schlajchtet Wada.

When the wolves howl, then bad weather's coming.

13-5 Wan et räajent enn de Sonn schient, dan haft de Wulf daut Feeba.

When it rains while the sun shines, then the wolf has fever (he is not at your door).

13-6 Owent—root,
Morje—goot.

Evening—red,
Morning—good.

13-7   Morje-stund
      Haft Golt emm "Mund."

Morning hour
Has gold in the mouth.

Early morn—
With gold adorned.

13-8   Wan et emm Winta kracht,
      Dan buschelt et emm Somma emm
         Sack.

When it in the winter bangs,
Then bushels it in the summer in
the sack.

When frost in winter goes crack,
Next summer's grain fills many a sack.

13-9   Aprell
      Deit waut hee well.

April
Does what it will.

The weather is unpredictable.

13-10 Daut's en Wada-profeet
      Dee fäl frat enn nuscht weet.

That's a weather prophet
Who much devours and nothing
   knows.

That's a weatherman for you—
Eating much and not a clue!

13-11 Aun Gottes Säajen
      Ess aules jeläajen.

On God's good tending
Is all now depending.

13-12 Daut rääjent,
      Gott säajent.

It rains,
God blesses.

It's raining,
God's reigning.

13-13 Kjast enn Hei-wada ess nijch aule
      Dach.

Weddings and good haying weather don't come every day. (Make hay while
the sun shines.)

13-14 Somma, audee;
      Scheide deit wee.

Summer, adieu;
Parting does hurt.

Summer, adieu—
Parting and rue.

13-15 Fe nu, daut meent säwen Joa.

For now, that means seven years (a lackadaisical attitude toward one's
commitments, a getting around to things one of these years).

13-16 Kjemt Tiet, kjemt Rot;
      Kjemt Sodel-tiet, kjemt Sot.

Comes time, comes solution;
Comes saddle [seeding] time,
comes seed.

In time comes needs,
Solutions, seeding, seeds.

All in good time.

13-17   Wäa sikj mett siene Pracharie nijch weet, ess nijch weat daut hee dee haft.

Who can't look after even his little bit, shouldn't have even that.

13-18   Oabeit moakt daut Läwe seet; Fulheit stoakjt de Jläda.

Work makes life sweet; laziness strengthens the limbs (a comment on life's paradoxes?).

FOURTEEN

Maxims About the Vicissitudes of Life

14-1   Nu ess Hopp enn Moll feloare.   Now hops and mash are lost. (All is lost.)

14-2   Hee kaun nijch emol dän Hunt utem Owe locke.   He can't even entice a dog to come out of the oven (because he's so down-and-out and doesn't have food enough).

14-3   De Lenj drajcht de Laust.   Time heals life's tribulations.

14-4   Wäa de Schode haft, dee woat dän Spott aul kjrieje.   Who has misfortune will also get ridicule.

14-5   Wan "wan" nijch wea, dan wea mauncha Bua en Adelmaun, enn en Adelmaun en Pracha.   If "if" were not, then were many a farmer a nobleman, and a nobleman a beggar.

14-6   Soo jeit et oppe Welt—
Eene haft dän Biedel;
De aundra haft daut Jelt.   So goes it on the world—
One has the purse;
The other has the money.   So things are in the world—
One man has the billfold;
The other has the gold.

14-7   Jlekj enn Glauss—woo boolt brakjt daut!   Luck and glass—how soon they break!

14-8   Hee haft meea Jlekj auss Festaunt.   He has more luck than brains.

14-9   Doa ess nuscht too hole, wua de   Nothing can be expected where the ruler has lost authority.
        Kjeisa daut Rajcht feloare haft.

14-10   Fonn Hoate enn Jenode—   From hearts and compassion—   For one's heartfelt compassion
        Fief Kjieltje enn sass Mode.   Five noodles and six maggots.   Five noodles is your ration.

        Do not expect to be rewarded for a kind deed.

14-11   De easchta Dach en Gaust,   The first day one's a guest,
        De äwaje Tiet ne Laust.   The remaining time a pest.

14-12   Wäa weet waut fonne Lus wie ons   Who knows what kind of louse we're thereby putting into our fur coat?
        doamett enn däm Pels sate.   (—what bee we're putting into our bonnet?)

14-13   Een jiedra moakt sien äjen Jeschekj.   Everyone makes his own destiny.

14-14   Eene woat oolt auss ne Koo   One gets as old as a cow
        Enn leat emma meea doa too.   And always learns more and more

14-15   Daut Ella kjemt nijch mett Jemack.   Growing old is not without discomfort.

14-16   Fe däm Doot ess kjeen Krut jewosse.   For death is no herb grown. (There is no cure for death.)

14-17   De Mana oabeide enn de Frues hiele.   Men work and women cry. (For men must work and women must weep.)

14-18   O jana jo,   O that one yes,   O yessiree,
        Woo jeit mie daut soo no!   How goes me that so close!   How much that touches me!

14-19   Wua daut Hoat fonn foll ess, doa jeit   From what fills one's heart, one's mouth overflows.
        daut Mul fonn äwa.

14-20   Hee wudd sikj de Heane noch auf   He'll wear off his horns in good time. (He'll get taken down a peg or two
        rane.   yet.)

14-21   De Jääja enn de Fescha senn emma   The hunter and the fisherman are always poor.
        oam.

14-22   Jelt, jelt,   Money, money,   Gold, gold,
        Schrijcht de gaunsse Welt.   Shrieks the whole world.   Cries the world.

14-23 Aules ess nijch Golt waut jäl schient.

All that glitters is not gold.

14-24 Am woat de Kost noch moaga woare.

The spendthrift will see leaner days.

14-25 Straum enn fedrisslijch; koddrijch enn lostijch.

Dressed-up and grumbly; ragged and happy.

14-26 Et jeft Mensche, Schiltkjräte, uck dreekauntje Fiele.

There are people, turtles, and three-cornered files. (It takes all kinds to make a world.)

14-27 De Mensch denkjt,
Oba Gott lenkjt.

Man proposes,
But God disposes.

14-28 Wää daut Kjriets haft, säajent sikj et easchte.

Who has the Cross (carries the Christian message) blesses himself first.

14-29 Aula Aunfank ess schwoa.

All beginnings are hard.

14-30 Spoa enne Tiet, dan hast enne Noot.

Spare in time, have when in need. (Save for a rainy day.)

14-31 Spoa enne Noot;
Wan du hast, dan frat goot.

Spare when in the need;
When you have, then devour good.

Spare when in need;
In good times, eat well indeed.

14-32 Ekj ät waut goa ess
Enn drinkj waut kloa ess.

I eat what done is
And drink what clear is.

I eat what is here
And drink what is clear.

14-33 Ne blinje Han finjt uck nochmol en goodet Kuarn.

A blind hen also finds a good kernel now and then.

14-34 Wan et nijch rääjent, dan kaun de oama Maun sien Hamd dräje.

If it doesn't rain, the poor man can at least dry his shirt.

14-35 En grootet Jeschrejch—
Enn en kjlienet Jerejcht!

A great shrieking—
And a small judgment!

A great big to-do
Over little to do!

14-36   En Droom ess en Droch,   A dream is a drug,   A dream is as naught,
        Emm Hamd ess en Loch,   In the shirt is a hole,   A shirt has a spot,
        Wea jistre enn ess uck noch.   Was yesterday and is also still.   Was there before, like as not.

Life goes on as it always has despite anyone's fancy notions.

14-37   Maun jeit derjch dikj enn denn.   Man goes through thick and thin (must take the bitter with the sweet).

14-38   Doawäajen woat noch kjeen Oss   On that account no ox will calve. (It is just not of much consequence.)
        kaulwe.

14-39   Wäa aunhelt, dee jewennt.   Who persists will succeed.

14-40   Lot nijch fuats daut Hoat enne   Don't let your heart slide down at once into your pants.
        Bekjse schorre.

14-41   Nijch fuats de Pistool emm Growe Don't throw away your pistol at once in the trench. (Don't give up the
        schmiete.   battle before it's started.)

14-42   Äwrem Hunt senn wie; nu mott wie We've got past the dog; now we still have to get past the tail. (The worst is
        noch äwrem (T)soagel.   over, but we're not out of the woods yet.)

14-43   Waut lang deat, woat entlijch.   What lasts a long time, at long last is done. (All things come to an end *or* All
                                          things come to those who wait.)

14-44   Daut ess soo lang trigj, daut ess That is so long ago, that it's hardly true anymore.
        meist nijch meea soo.

14-45   Jelenja, jeschlemma.   The longer, the poorer.

14-46   Jelenja, jeleewa.   The longer, the better. (The longer the anticipation, the sweeter the
                                          realization.)

14-47   Daut deat en Stoot;   That takes a time;   It takes a while;
        Doafäa woat et dan uck goot.   Therefore becomes it then also good.   Then will it be done in style.

14-48   Aules haft en Enj; blooss de Worscht   Everything comes to an end—except a sausage. It comes to two ends.
        haft twee Enja.

14-49   Enj goot, aules goot!   All's well that ends well.

FIFTEEN

Maxims About Daily Behavior

15-1	Wan aul, dan aul.	If at all, then all the way! (What's worth doing at all is worth doing well.)
15-2	Eene mott sikj too halpe weete.	One has to know how to help himself.
15-3	Fonn nuscht ess nuscht.	From nothing comes nothing.
15-4	Nuscht jewoagt, nuscht jewonne.	Nothing ventured, nothing gained.
15-5	Fresch jewoagt ess haulf jewonne.	Fresh begun is half done.
15-6	Wäa säkjt, dee finjt.	Who seeks, will find.
15-7	Daut halpt nuscht daut Mul spetse; daut mott jepiept woare.	It helps nothing just to pucker the lips; you have to whistle.
15-8	Meed haft sikj opp jehunge.	Tiredness has hanged itself. (Now is no time to be tired.)
15-9	Enn Russlaunt froag wie nijch no Meed.	In Russia we don't question whether we're tired or not.
15-10	Nuscht mett Haust auss Huppsfläje jriepe.	Nothing with haste except catching fleas.

15-11   Wäa stoakj febie foat, dee sitt daut nijch; enn wäa sacht foat, dee jleeft daut mott soo.

Who drives by fast, doesn't see it; and who drives by slowly thinks that's how it should be. (Do not be self-centered about appearances—others do not even notice.)

15-12   Rejchttoo ess noda; runtomm jeit eea.

Cutting across is closer; going the long way around is faster.

15-13   Daut jeit.

That'll pass muster.

15-14   Wäa et nijch emm Kopp haft, haft et enne Feet.

Who doesn't use his head must use his feet.

15-15   Jeleada, jefekjeada.

The more school, the more fool.

15-16   Nieschea haft de Welt fedorwe.

Curiosity has spoiled the world. (Curiosity killed the cat.)

15-17   Haunteare deit leare.

Doing means learning. (Practice makes perfect.)

15-18   Onnfesocht sprakjt onnbedocht.

Inexperience bespeaks thoughtlessness.

15-19   En Boom ess niemols too oolt toom bäje.

A tree is never too old to bend.

15-20   En oola Hunt ess schwoa bale leare.

It's hard to teach an old dog to bark. (You can't teach an old dog new tricks.)

15-21   En Hunt lat fonne Hoa, oba nijch fonne Nekje.

A dog loses its hair but not its peculiarities.

15-22   Et ess kjeene Schaund dol too faule, oba ligje bliewe ess.

It is no shame to fall down, only to stay down.

15-23   Junk jedone, oolt bedocht.

Youthful actions, old reflections.

15-24   Mett däm Hoot enne Haunt Kjemt Maun derjch daut gaunsse Launt.

With the hat in the hand, Comes man through the whole land.

With his hat in his hand, Man's welcome throughout the land.

15-25   Wunde fonn Wead senn schwoa too heele.

Wounds from words are slow to heal.

15-26   Fe däm go ekj nijch een Schrett äwaroasch.

For him I won't go one step backwards (—won't backdown).

15-27   De Kjläkjsta jeft no.

The wisest gives in.

15-28   Wäa wellijch jeft, jeft dobbelt.

Who gives willingly, gives doubly.

15-29   Fespräakje ess "ehrlich,"
Hoole ess "schwerlich."

Promising is honorable,
Holding is difficult.

To promise is good;
The keeping is hard.

15-30   Wan eene eenmol lijcht,
Däm jleeft Maun nijch—
Enn wan hee uck de Woarheit sajcht.

When one once lies,
Him believes man not—
And if he also the truth says.

When man once lies,
Then no matter how hard he tries,
His truthfulness will not be prized.

15-31   Selfst lowe stinkjt.

Self-praise reeks.

15-32   Däm fält en bät too beschliepe.

His sharp corners need grinding down a bit. (He needs to be put in his place.)

15-33   Däm fält too behäwle.

He needs to be planed (that is, with a carpenter's plane).

Nos. 32 and 33 mean pretty much the same. In English we use the terms "rough edges" and "being polished," but these refer to the social graces. Mennonites are talking of, and more concerned with, one's moral behavior.

15-34   Däm woa ekj de Glooja läse.

I'll read him the riot act.

15-35   Daut Peat weet wua siene Kjrebb ess.

A horse knows its own crib (people too should know where they belong).

15-36   Wua kjeen Kloaga ess, ess uck kjeen Rejchta.

Where there's no complainer, there's also no judge.

15-37   Auf ekj well ooda nijch, ekj mott.

If I want to or not, I must. (Duty calls.)

15-38   Daut ess jedan auss en jiedra daut jleijcht.

Everyone to his own taste.

15-39   Dee luat daut am de jebrodne Jans sulle emm Hauls fläje.

He's waiting for geese, already roasted, to fly into his mouth.

15-40   Wäa sikj nijch saut jejäte haft, dee woat sikj nohäa aul nijch saut lekje.

Who hasn't eaten enough will not get sated later by just licking.

15-41   Wäa tiedijch oppsteit, kjemt too waut.

Who rises early, comes to something (makes something of himself).

15-42   En bät too lot ess fäl too lot.

A bit too late is much too late.

15-43   Hee haft sikj daut Bad jemoakt; dan mott hee uck doabenne schlope.

He's made his own bed; now he must sleep in it.

15-44   Hee haft sikj de Mooss ennjereat; dan mott hee dee uck ut äte.

He's stirred up his own *Mooss*; now he must also eat it.

15-45   Ne Kaut emm Sack soll eene nijch kjeepe.

One shouldn't buy a cat in a sack (a pig in a poke).

15-46   Frintlijche Hunjtjes biete uck.

Friendly little dogs bite too.

15-47   Wäa sikj enn Jefoa jeft, kjemt enn Jefoa omm.

Who lives dangerously, dies dangerously.

15-48   Nu ess miene Mot foll.

Now is my measure full. (Enough's enough—I've had it up to here.)

15-49   Wäa daut kjliene nijch eat.
        Ess daut groote nijch weat.

Who the little thing not honors,   Who holds the little of no worth
Is the great thing not worth.   Is never worthy of the great.

SIXTEEN

Comparisons

16-1	—truhoatijch auss ne Mutta	—as conscientious (true-hearted) as a mother
16-2	—opprejchtijch auss en Foda	—as honest (upright) as a father
16-3	—fonn onnjefäa soo auss wan de Bua Plume at	—more or less, like a farmer eating plums
16-4	—at auss en Drascha	—eats like a thresher
16-5	—meea auss de "Polizei" erlaubt	—more than the police allow (than the law allows)
16-6	—fäasejchtijch auss Blauwboat	—as foresighted as Bluebeard
16-7	—rant auss en Schäare-schliepa	—runs like a scissors grinder
16-8	—feschwinjt auss en (T)sejon enne lange Nacht	—vanishes like a gypsy into the long night
16-9	Opp Temmamaun's Hoabreet kjemt et nijch d'ropp aun, enn daut ess auss been-dikj.	To a carpenter a hairbreadth doesn't matter, and to him that hairbreadth may be as thick as a leg. (It doesn't matter whatever way you look at it.)
16-10	—rät auss en Schnieda	—talks like a tailor

16-11 —rät soo auss am de Mets sett   —talks so that his cap will fit him best (talks to his own advantage)

16-12 —paust auss Auntje too Mets   —fits like little Anna's cap (fits to a T)

16-13 —paust auss en Sodel oppe Säaj   —fits like a saddle on a sow (not appropriate or becoming)

16-14 —haft de Welle auss en Hunt emm Borm   —has as much freedom as a dog in a well

16-15 Wan en dobbel Schläde nijch jleist, sitt daut auss wan en Hunt too Kjast jeit.   If a bobsleigh doesn't trail properly (this is, if the back runners don't follow in the front tracks), it looks like a dog going to a wedding.

16-16 —schmock auss en auf-jelekjta Kota   —as nice as a licked-over tomcat

16-17 —sittet soo auss wan en Kota mett de Worscht auf jeit   —looks like a tomcat who walks away with the sausage

16-18 —schaftijch auss en derjch-jehauwda Kota   —happy as a thoroughly thrashed tomcat

16-19 —schaftijch auss en Fesch emm Wota   —happy as a fish in water

16-20 —schaftijch auss en Topptje Mies   —happy as a pot of mice (presumably fallen into the pot, unable to get out, and anything but happy)

16-21 —oam auss ne Kjoakje Mus   —poor as a church mouse

16-22 —ritt äwaroasch auss ne nekjsche Schrugg   —pulls backwards (that is, acts contrary) like a stubborn nag

16-23 —weet soo fäl doafonn auss ne oole Koo fonn Sinndach   —knows as much about it as does an old cow about Sunday

16-24 —weet soo fäl doafonn auss ne Koo fonne Mon   —knows as much about it as a cow about the moon

16-25 Jieda Dach emm Niejoa woat soo fäl lenja auss en Hon's jekjrei.

Each succeeding day in the new year becomes as much longer as the time taken up by a rooster's crowing.

16-26 —sett doa auss ne Ent oppem Stobbe

—sits there like a duck on a stump (doesn't know which way to turn)

16-27 —sett doa auss en Klots

—sits there like a block of wood

16-28 —at auss en Rogga-wulf

—eats like a rye-wolf

16-29 —jinkj auss heete Brie

—went like hot mush (like hotcakes)

16-30 —spetst ut auss Lamkje sien Meddach

—comes to nothing like Lemke's dinner

16-31 —onnmäajlijch auss Kjieltje ute Kruck äte

—impossible as eating noodles out of a jug

16-32 —läft auss ne Mod emm Schmäa

—lives like a maggot in grease (lives richly)

16-33 —läft auss Kjlien'-gott enn "Frankreich"

—lives like a little god in France

16-34 —hinjaraun auss ne Iel nom Bloot

—persistent as a leech after blood

16-35 —haft et rut auss de Pracha ne Lus

—has a knack for it as a beggar does for lice

16-36 —nuscht weat auss toom emm Glausschaup sate

—worth nothing but to set in a glass showcase

16-37 —aula enn ne Räj auss Kloses' Kjäj

—all in a row like Klaassens' cows

16-38 —jlikj wajch auss ne Bottamalkj's Wies

—monotonous like a buttermilk tune

16-39 —kolt auss ne baustne Lusch

—cold as a bag made of bark

16-40 —domm auss Bonestroo

—crazy as beanstalks

16-41   —hendijch auss en Schwenjel aum   —handy as a crank on an overcoat
        Äwarock

16-42   —dreit sikj auss ne Wintmäl   —turns about like a windmill (said of one who thinks overly much of her
                                                 own beauty and in displaying it)

SEVENTEEN

Other Expressions

17-1   Kort enn dikj haft kjeen Jeschekj; lank enn denn haft uck kjeen Senn.

Short-and-fat's not much for shape, but sense there's none in tall-and-thin.

17-2   Hee ess nijch oppem Kopp jefolle.

He has not fallen on his head. (He is not stupid.)

17-3   Hee ess nijch fonn jistre.

He wasn't born yesterday.

17-4   Hee weet fonn wua de Wint pust.

He knows from where the wind blows. (He cannot be fooled.)

17-5   Hee weet woo de Forkj emm Stäl stakjt.

He knows which end of the handle the fork is on. (He knows the score.)

17-6   Hee weet waut am jebrode ess.

He knows what's fried for him. (He knows what's in store.)

17-7   Hee weet goot wua Lucks Beea holt.

He well knows where *Lucks* gets beer. (He knows what it's all about.)

17-8   Hee woat mie kjeene Brell fekjeepe.

He won't sell me any glasses (wont't sell me a bill of goods *or* I won't let the wool be pulled over my eyes).

The person won't let himself be "sold" any glasses which will make him see an unreal picture.

17-9   Hee ess nijch oppem Mul jefolle.

He hasn't fallen on his mouth. (He's got something to say.)

17-10	Hee weet sien Schoptje too schäare.	He knows how to shear his sheep. (He knows how to get the longest end of the stick.)
17-11	Hee haft en Noagel emm Kopp.	He has a nail in his head. (He's a know-it-all.)
17-12	Am ess ne Späkj looss.	He's got a loose spoke.
17-13	Hee ess fonne Koo jebäte.	He's bitten by a cow. (He doesn't know beans.)
17-14	Hee ess nijch bie de fiew.	He's out of his (five) senses.
17-15	Hee sajcht nijch buff noch muff.	He says neither yea nor nay.
17-16	Hee ess een Post-sack too lot.	He's one mailbag too late (just missed the boat).
17-17	Hee deit daut äwa Hauls enn Kopp.	He does that over neck and head (does that lickety-split).
17-18	Daut ess too seea oppe Not.	That's too much on the seam. (That's being too fussy.)
17-19	Hee at mett lange Täne.	He eats with long teeth (is squeamish).
17-20	Mett am ess nijch goot Kjieltje äte.	He's not a person to eat noodles with. (He's hard to get along with.)
17-21	Hee haft Tint jesope.	He's been drinking ink. (He's way out of line.)
17-22	Waut dient ess, ess mient; waut mient ess, daut kjemmat die nuscht.	What yours is, is mine; what mine is, is none of your business.
17-23	Hee kaun aules habe waut de Heena laje, blooss de Eia nijch.	He can have anything the chickens lay, only not the eggs (that is, he can't have anything).
17-24	Hee haft de Korf jekjrääje.	He got the basket (his marriage proposal was turned down).
17-25	See naume am toom jreene Donnadach.	They gave him green Thursday.
		They chastised him—a meeting of church fathers decided upon chastisement of wrongdoers.

17-26	Däm woare de Scheestje weppe.	His coattails will go flapping. (He will go packing.)
17-27	Hee ess huntmeed.	He is dog-tired.
17-28	Nu stone de Osse aum Boajch.	Now stand his oxen at the foot of a hill. (He's at wits' end.)
17-29	Am stone de Hoa too Boaj.	His hair stands on end. (He's scared out of his wits.)
17-30	Hee haft ne hoade Nät too knacke.	He has a hard nut to crack.
17-31	Däm ess et fonne Paun jebrennt.	He's gone from the frying pan into the fire.
17-32	Nu ess hee enne Mooss.	Now he's in a *Mooss* (in a stew).
17-33	Daut ess oba ne Rea-mooss.	That is ever a stirred-up *Mooss*. (What a mix-up!)
17-34	Nu ess de Topp twei.	Now is the pot broken. (Now things have come to a breaking point.)
17-35	Daut ess nijch oppe holle Tän.	That's not enough to fill a hollow tooth.
17-36	Hee haft nijch Solt oppem Ei.	He hasn't salt for his egg. (He's down and out.)
17-37	Hee ess kjriesel-runt.	He's in a whirling tizzy.
17-38	Dee schlope aula unja eene Dakj.	They all sleep under the same blanket.
17-39	Nu ess hundat enn eent ut.	Now it's beyond hundred and one. (That's the last straw *or* That's enough.)
17-40	Hee piept utem latste Loch.	He's piping out of the last hole (piping his last tune—he's at his last resort).
17-41	Nu ess am de Mot foll.	For him the measure is now full. (He's had it up to here.)
17-42	Daut jrebbelt enn jäat.	That bubbles and boils (with people). [*jäare*: to ferment]
17-43	Am rant de Gaul äwa.	His gall is boiling over (with anger).

17-44 Hee woat sikj nijch lote emm Bock's Huarn joage.

He won't let himself be driven against the ram's horns. (He won't let himself be backed into a corner.)

17-45 Hee woat mettem Kopp derjch de Waunt foare.

He'll drive his head through the wall. (He's bull-headed.)

17-46 See haft en Bock emm Rock.

She has a ram in her skirt (is headstrong and tries to butt her way into things).

17-47 See well de Bekjse droage.

She wants to wear the pants.

17-48 Hee ess nijch fonn (T)socka.

He's not made of sugar. (He can take it.)

17-49 Hee haft Hoa oppe Täne.

He has hair on his teeth. (He's no pushover.)

17-50 Däm woa ekj unja feea Ooge seene.

I'll have a four-eyed meeting with him (tell him off face-to-face).

17-51 Hee ess kort romme Akj.

He is fast around corners (abrupt in his speech).

17-52 Däm haud hee ne goode Schnuts jejäft.

He gave him a good snootful (told him off).

17-53 Hee woat Rosmack-hoole.

He'll clean house (metaphorically)!

17-54 Hee woat Donnadach hoole.

He's going to hold Thursday (going to clean house around here).

17-55 Daut ess mau jemoakt no Näs enn Mul.

That is done only by nose and mouth (only after a fashion).

17-56 Hee deit daut mett henje enn warje.

He does that only with a hanging and choking (only with great pains).

17-57 Dan jeft et en Kotadauns.

That will give a tomcat dance (will stir up a hornets' nest).

17-58 Ditt ess ut Raunt enn Baunt.

This is out of bounds and bonds (out of hand).

17-59 Wan aule Strenj riete, dan haft hee Fräd.

When all ropes tear, then he has peace. (When everything goes to pieces, at least it's past worrying about.)

17-60 Daut woat hee aum Schorsteen schriewe.

He'll write it on the chimney (record it so that it will be forgotten about—for example, a debt).

17-61	Hee haft ne Fiastäd.	He has a farmstead (that is, a place to keep warm).
17-62	Hee haft ne Krupunja.	He has a place to creep under (that is, a roof over his head).
17-63	Am felt en Steen fomm Hoat.	A stone falls off his heart. (That's a load off his mind.)
17-64	Kolde Haunt, woamet Hoat.	Cold hand, warm heart.
17-65	Lang nijch jeseene enn doch noch jekjant.	Long time no see but still familiar.
17-66	Hee head daut derjche Bloom.	He heard it through a flower (through the grapevine).
17-67	Daut woat am emm Buck kjittle.	That will tickle his belly (tickle his funny bone).
17-68	Daut woat am emm Buck biete.	That will bite his belly (grip his funny bone).
17-69	Am spekjt de Howa.	He's feeling his oats.
		He feels spunky as a horse does when fed on oats.
17-70	Au-wee!	Ou-ouch!
17-71	Ach Mensch!	Ah man!
17-72	Mein-(t)seit!	Oh, my!
17-73	Hots-dusent!	*Hots*-thousand! (an expression of great surprise)
17-74	Dusent noch eent!	A thousand and one! (an expression of even greater surprise)
17-75	Dusent mol nä!	A thousand times no!
17-76	Ie-waut!	Can't be! (an expression of disbelief)
17-77	Huj-uj-uj!	My, my, my! (Hoity-toity!)

EIGHTEEN

One-Word Characterizations

18-1 Frauts (face-maker)—mischievous boy

18-2 Kjrietsspaun (cross-span, spider)—rambunctious child

18-3 Breslinkj—ornery child

18-4 Laups—dolt

18-5 Koddajalaups—ragged dolt

18-6 Rietspliet (tear-_____)—ragamuffin

18-7 Schnigjelfrits (_____-Fritz)—cute little fellow

18-8 Wrauntasack (wriggle-sack)—restless baby

18-9 Piepedakjsel (pipe-lid)—affectionate bantering term for a child

18-10 Oole-schlorr (old wooden sandal)—argumentative woman

18-11 Oole-näs (old nose)—affected precocious child

18-12 Topptje-kjikja (little pot looker)—nosey child

18-13 Junga-schnäakja—young smart-aleck

18-14 Brauselmauts—know-it-all woman

18-15 Pludakott (gossip-_____)—gossip

18-16 Klotjedroaga (cote-carrier)—rumor-monger

18-17 Teewehakjs (_____-witch)—scold

18-18 Struckhakjs (brush-witch)—hag

18-19 Pukja (pig)—slovenly woman

18-20 Os (carrion)—detestable person

18-21 Oole-kjrät (old toad)—old hag

18-22 Os-kjrät (carrion-toad)—repulsive hag

18-23 Kjeadel (variation of "Karl" or "Carl")—stalwart person

18-24 Sonda-klooka (remarkably wise man)—genius

18-25 Näajen-klooka (nine-wise man)—clever person

18-26 Ulespäjel (owls-mirror)—wit

18-27 Dusent-kjensla (thousand-performer)—jack-of-all-trades

18-28 Nootnoagel (need-nail)—put-upon person

18-29 Poslacka—joe-boy

18-30 Beräajenda-hon (rained-on rooster)—bumpkin

18-31 Drän(t)soagel (drone-tail)—scramble-brained person

18-32 Schlusjon—not very bright person

18-33 Dommajon (crazy-_____)—simpleton

18-34 Dwautschhauns (deranged Hans)—deranged person

18-35   Haunsworscht (Hans-sausage)—clown

18-36   Dusel—wishy-washy person

18-37   Weekjbroot (soft bread)—backboneless person

18-38   Stremp (stocking)—milquetoast

18-39   Doojaus—lackadaisical person

18-40   Langsomma-meddach (slow-dinner)—slowpoke

18-41   Fula-äsel (lazy donkey)—lazy person

18-42   Domma-äsel (crazy donkey)—bad individual

18-43   Schladonss—slovenly person

18-44   Schlopmets (sleepy cap)—forgetful person

18-45   Schlosäwendoot (slay-seven-dead)—do-nothing

18-46   Nikjsnuts (nothing-useful)—good-for-nothing

18-47   Kjnirps (dwarf)—twirp

18-48   Jreenschnowel (green-beak)—greenhorn

18-49   Unjadont—underling

18-50   Sotstrunk (seed-stalk)—one who falls short of
        expectations

18-51   Rommdriewa (around-driver)—gadabout

18-52   Supknust (drink-bump)—souse

18-53   Oola-knacks (old-crack)—old man

18-54   Jriessjräm (dirty complainer)—grumbler

18-55   Grommsauja—complainer

18-56   Suatopp (sour pot)—sourpuss

18-57   Dollstock (angry stick)—sorehead

18-58   Domma-bädel (crazy scoundrel)—nasty person

18-59   Jietspungel (stingy-sack)—tightwad

18-60   Jietskjniepa (stingy pincher)—penny pincher

18-61   Schlorre-kaptein (wooden-shoe captain)—very
        minor official or bureaucrat

18-62   Spetsbub (pointed boy)—thief

18-63   Hollunk—rascal

18-64   Loosslada (loose-leather)—small-time con-artist

18-65   Heltabless (wooden blaze)—thick-skinned person

18-66   Drepsdrell—no-account

18-67   Niescheaje-op (curious ape)—extremely
        inquisitive person

18-68   Fielfros (much-devourer)—glutton

18-69   Flakjfeeba (intestine-fever)—pest

18-70   Stiakopp (steer-head)—bullheaded person

18-71   Dommkopp (crazy-head)—blockhead

18-72   Dikjkopp (thick-head)—person thick between the
        ears

18-73   Dwautschkop (deranged-head)—really deranged
        person

18-74   Nätkopp (nut-head)—nut

18-75   Blottkop (mud-head)—gowk

18-76   Dränkopp (drone-head)—witless person

18-77   Blajchkopp (tin-head)—empty-headed person

18-78   Plumpskopp (drop-head)—scatterbrain

18-79   Glomskopp (cottage-cheesehead)—brainless
        person

18-80   Schopskopp (sheep-head)—dunderhead

18-81   Belkjhauls (yell-throat)—screamer

18-82   Jietshauls (stingy throat)—miser

18-83   Haulftän (half-tooth)—one with chip on her
        shoulder

18-84   Räpeltän (_____-tooth)—"cracked" person

18-85   Mäakjeltän (fussy-tooth)—overly fussy person

18-86   Jältän (yellow-tooth)—bogeyman

18-87   Plaupamul—prattlemouth

18-88   Blaubafrät (babble-animal mouth)— blabber-
        mouth

18-89   Grootfrät (big animal mouth)—big-mouth

Appendix

GRAMMAR AND USAGE

ARTICLES/PRONOUNS

the—de(e) (masc. nom., all fem., all pl.) (*de* is unaccented
    form)
    däm (masc. dat., occasionally neut. dat. and masc. acc.)
    dän (masc. acc.)
    daut (all neut.) (sometimes shortened to *et*)
a—e(e)n (all masc. and neut.) (*en* is unaccented form)
    e(e)ne (all fem.) (usually shortened to unaccented *ne*)

NOTE: The definite article forms above (with the addition of
    däa and *waut*) are also used as a kind of personal pronoun
    or relative pronoun as follows:
he, she, they, who—dee
him—däm
her—däa
it—daut/et
which, that—daut/waut
them—dän

NOTE: The indefinite article form above is also used for the in-
    definite pronoun as follows:
one—eena (masc. nom.)
    eenem (masc. dat./acc.)
    eene (fem.)
    eent (neut.)

DEMONSTRATIVE PRONOUNS

this—disa (masc. nom.; adj.—*diss*)
    disem (masc. dat./acc.; adj.—*diss/disen*)
    dise (all fem.)
    ditt (all neut.)

that—jana (masc. nom.; adj.—*jan*)
    janem (masc. dat./acc.; adj.—*jan/janen*)
    jane (all fem.)
    jant (neut.; adj.—*jan*)
these—dise
those—jane

PERSONAL PRONOUNS

I—ekj   me—mie
we—wie   us—ons
you—du (nom. sing.; formal—*see/jie*)
    die (dat./acc. sing.; formal—*an/ju* or *junt*)
    jie (nom. pl.)
    ju/junt (dat./acc. pl.)
he—hee   him—am
she—see   her—äa
they—see   them—an
it—et
himself, herself, itself, themselves—sikjselfst

POSSESSIVE ADJECTIVES/PRONOUNS

NOTE: These take no endings (except -*e*—all fem. and pl. only)
    when there is a following noun. When there is no following
    noun, the endings are -*a* (masc. nom.), -*en* (masc.
    dat./acc.), -*e* (all fem. and pl.), -*t* (all neut.) (notice that
    äa + -*e* becomes *äare*; *äa* + -*a* remains *äa*).
my (mine)—mien   our(s)—ons
yours(s) (sing.)—dien (formal—*äa/jun*)
your(s) (pl.)—jun
his—sien   her(s)—äa
its—sien   their(s)—äa

INTERROGATIVE PRONOUNS

who—wäa   whom—wäm
whose—wäms
which (one)—woon (endings as in possessive pronouns
   above)
what—waut   when—waneea
why—wauromm   how—woo

SAMPLES OF VERB FORMS

1. *Anomalous Verbs*
be—senne; past participle—jewast/jewäse
    Pres. sing.—ekj sie, du best, hee ess; pl.—(wie, jie, see)
       senn
    Past sing.—ekj wea, du weascht, hee wea; pl.—weare
do—doone; past participle—jedone
    Pres. sing.—ekj doo, du deist, hee deit; pl.—doone
    Past sing.—ekj deed, du deedst, hee deed; pl.—deede
go—gone; past participle—jegone
    Pres. sing.—ekj go, du jeist, hee jeit; pl.—gone
    Past sing.—ekj jinkj, du jinkjst, hee jinkj; pl.—jinje

2. *Weak Verbs*
run—rane; past participle—jerant
    Pres. sing.—ekj ran, du ranst, hee rant; pl.—rane
    Past sing.—ekj rand, du randst, hee rand; pl.—rande
have—habe; past participle—jehaut
    Pres. sing.—ekj ha, du hast, hee haft; pl.—habe
    Past sing.—ekj haud, du haudst, hee haud; pl.—haude
think—denkje; past participle—jedocht
    Pres. sing.—ekj denkj, du denkjst, hee denkjt; pl.—
       denkje
    Past sing.—ekj docht, du dochst, hee docht; pl.—
       dochte

3. *Strong Verbs*
come—kome; past participle—jekome
    Pres. sing.—ekj kom, du kjemst, hee kjemt; pl.—kome
    Past sing.—ekj kjeem, du kjeemst, hee kjeem;
       pl.—kjeeme

OTHER COMMON VERBS

to live—läwe	to laugh—lache
to die—stoawe	to cry—hiele
to work—schaufe, oabeide	to want—welle
to sleep—schlope	to play—späle
to get up—oppstone	to read—läse
to stand—stone	to write—schriewe
to sit—sette	to paint—foawe
to look—kjikje	to sing—sinje
to see—seene	to ride—riede
to hear—heare	to visit—spatseare
to smell—rikje	to stay—bliewe
to taste—schmakje	to keep—hoole
to drink—drinkje	to give—jäwe
to eat—äte	to buy—kjeepe
to cook—koake	to sell—fekjeepe
to fry—brode	to begin—aunfange
to bake—backe	to end—oppheare
to wash—wausche	to burn—brenne
to sew—neie	to help—halpe
to say—saje	to become—woare
to learn—leare	to farm—foarmre
to know—weete	to sow—seie
to teach—leare	to grow—wausse
to preach—prädje	to rain—rääjne
to pray—bäde	to snow—schniea
to believe—jleewe	to thank—danke

COMMON ADVERBS

NOTE: Many adjectives (see later), without any alteration,
   also serve as adverbs.

yes—yo	very—seea
no—nä	too—too
not—nijch	much—fäl
never—niemols	indeed—woll
only—blooss	now—nu
sometimes—majchmol	soon—boolt
often—foaken	then—dan
always—emma	again—wada
here—hia	there—han
there—doa	back—trigj
approximately—onnjefäa	

ADVERBS/PREPOSITIONS

NOTE: These all are declined similarly to the first example, but only some have an intensive form. The dative endings include the article "the" (*oppem Peat* = on the horse).

on (or upon)—opp (adv.)
        oppem (masc. and neut. dat.)
        oppe (fem. and pl. dat.)
        (e)nopp (when obj. of prep. is understood; also as intensive)

out—ut, utem, ute, (e)rut
at (or up to)—aun, aunem or aum, aune, (e)naun
in—enn, emm, enne (e)nenn
in front of—fäa, fäarem, fäare
behind—hinja, hinjrem, hinjre
beside or by—bie, biem, bie
around—romm, rommem, romme, (e)romm
over—äwa, äwrem, äwre
under—unja, unjrem, unjre
above—bowa, bowrem, bowre
off—auf, _____, _____, (e) rauf
with—mett, mettem, mette
between—tweschen
among—mank, mankem, manke, mank
after—no, nom
for—fe
from—fonn, fomm, fonne
through—derjch, derjchem, derjche, derjch
to—no, nom (with obj.)
    too, toom (with v.)
    bat (e.g., 1 *bat* 10)

COMMON ADJECTIVES

NOTE: These take endings of *-a* (all masc. nom.), *-en* or *-e/-a* (all masc. dat./acc.), *-e* (all fem. and pl., weak neut.), *-et* (strong neut.). Comparatives are formed with an ending of *-a*, superlatives with an ending of *-ste* (in some instances the adjective may undergo a vowel change as well). It has been pointed out elsewhere that many adjectives, without any alteration, also serve as adverbs.

big—groot	wet—naut
small—kjlien	dry—dräjch
thick—dikj	hot—heet
thin—denn	cold—kolt
wide—breet	new—nie
narrow—schmaul	worn-out—februckt
long—lank	young—junk
short—kort	old—oolt
round—runt	light—leijcht
square—feakauntijch	heavy—schwoa
hard—hoat	bright—dach
soft—wäkj	dark—dunkel
high—hooch/huach	multi-colored—bunt
low—läjch	light-colored—lijcht
empty—ladijch	good—goot
full—foll	bad—schlajcht
sweet—seet	clever—klook/kluak
sour—sua	stupid—dwautsch
right—rajcht	rich—rikj
wrong—onnrajcht	poor—oam
left—lingsch	healthy—jesunt
tired—meed	sick—krank
strong—stoakj	angry—doll
weak—schwack	peaceful—frädlijch
loud—lud	satisfied—toofräd
quiet—stell	lazy—ful
early—tiedijch	logy—looj
late—lot	crazy—domm
clean—rein	happy—schaftijch
dirty—onnrein	sad—truarijch
honest—opprejchtijch	deep—deep
dishonest—onnopp- rejchtijch	shallow—flack

CONJUNCTIONS

and—enn	when—auls
but—oba	before—eea
or—ooda	until—bat
so—aulsoo	while—wiels
because—wiels, ommdaut	as—auss
in order that—omm	where—wua
if—wan	yet—noch

PLURALS

As in English, they are formed in a number of ways:
1. no ending—Fesch (fish)—Fesch
2. -s ending—Kuffel (cup)—Kuffels
3. -sch ending—Homa (hammer)—Homasch
4. -a ending—Ei (egg)—Eia
5. -e ending—Kaut (cat)—Kaute
6. vowel change—Foot (foot)—Feet
7. vowel change plus -a ending—Book/Buak (book)—Bäkja

POSSESSIVES

These are formed with the dative case plus possessive pronoun (or, less commonly, with preposition *fonn*). Example: the farmer's house— *däm Foarma sien Hus* (or, *daut Hus fonn däm Foarma*).

DIMINUTIVES

These take the ending -*tje*. Nouns ending in *k* have just the -*je* added. Example: *Hus—Hustje* (little house), *Buck—Buckje* (little belly).

BASIC VOCABULARY

NOTE: For purposes of practical reference, the items have been arranged not alphabetically but in groups of related subject matter. Even within the groups the arrangement tries to proceed in a logical fashion.

PEOPLE

people—Lied
human being—Mensch
man—Maun
woman—Frumensch
baby—Bäbe

child—Kjint
boy—Jung
girl—Mejal, Mäakje
bride—Brut
bridegroom—Briegaum

ONE'S BODY

body—Kjarpa
head—Kopp
hair—Hoa
face—Jesejcht
forehead—Stearn
eye—Oog/Uag
ear—Ua
nose—Näs
cheek—Back
mouth—Mul
lip—Lepp
tooth—Tän
tongue—Tung
chin—Kjenn
neck—Hauls
blood—Bloot

chest—Brost
heart—Hoat
lung—Lung
stomach—Moaga/Moag
belly—Buck
lap—Schoot
seat—Sett
limb—Jlett
bone—Knoake
arm—Oarm
hand—Haunt
finger—Finja
thumb—Dume
leg—Been
foot—Foot
toe—Tee

RELATIVES

relative—Frintschoft	grandfather—Grootfoda
father—Foda	grandmother—Grootmutta
mother—Mutta	grandchild—Grootkjint
husband—Maun	grandson—Grootsän
wife—Fru, Wief	granddaughter—Grootdochta
son—Sän	uncle—Onkel
daughter—Dochta	aunt—Taunte
brother—Brooda	cousin (male)—Fada
sister—Sesta	cousin (female)—Nijcht
sibling—Jeschwista	

OCCUPATIONS

occupation—Hauntwoakj	carpenter—Temmamaun
farmer—Bua, Foarma	preacher—Prädja
hired man—Kjnajcht	teacher—Schoolleara
worker—Oabeida	doctor—Docta
maid—Kjäakjsche	cowherd—Feehoad
babysitter—Kjinjamäakje	

BUILDINGS

building—Jebied	granary—Spicka
house—Hus	barn—Staul
summerkitchen—Sommakjäakj	school—School
smokehouse—Räkjahus	church—Kjoakj
outhouse—Bekjhus	store—Stua
smithy—Schmäd	windmill—Wintmäl

HOUSING

chimney—Schorsteen	wallpaper—Wauntpapea
roof—Dack	paint—Foaw
shingle—Schindel	door—Däa
stairs—Trap	window—Fensta
ceiling—Bän	windowsill—Fenstakopp
board—Brat	floor—Flua
wall—Waunt	carpet—Teppijch

ROOMS		
	room—Stow	cellar—Kjalla
	kitchen—Kjäakj	leanto—Owesied
	pantry—Koma	porch—Fäaleew
	diningroom—Ätstow	front porch—Fäatus
	livingroom—Grootestow	back porch—Hinjatus
	bedroom—Schlopstow	

FURNISHINGS		
	picture—Bilt	blanket—Dakj
	calendar—Kollenda	pillow—Kjesse
	curtain—Gerdien	pillowcase—Kjessebia
	blind—Raloo	sheets—Footloake
	tablecloth—Deschdakj	mattress—Madrauts
	bedspread—Badspreed	

FURNITURE		
	furniture—Meeble	lamp—Laump
	table—Desch	clock—Klock
	chair—Stool	cupboard—Äteschaup
	highchair—Kjinjastool	china cabinet—Glausschaup
	bench—Benkj	wardrobe—Kjleedaschaup
	sofa—Soofa	dresser—Komood
	stove—Owe	chest—Kjist
	kitchen range—Koakowe	bed—Bad
	heater—Hettowe	

KITCHENWARE		
	dishes—Teetijch	can—Kaun
	cup—Kuffel	big bowl—Komm
	saucer—Schatel	collander—Lajchakomm
	cup and saucer—Tauss	pot—Grope
	glass—Glauss	cauldron—Meagrope
	soup bowl—Kommtje	jug—Kruck
	plate—Schiew	pail—Ama
	knife—Massa	crock—Steentopp
	fork—Gaufel	churn—Bottafaut
	tablespoon—Ätlapel	potato masher—Brie-staumpa
	teaspoon—Teelapel	salt shaker—Solt-streia
	ladle—Schleef	flour sifter—Mäl Säw
	dipper—Schaptje	rolling pin—Rollholt
	frying pan—Paun	coffee mill—Koffemäl
	baking pan—Plot	

SEASONINGS

seasoning—Kjriedarie
salt—Solt
pepper—Päpa
mustard—Samp
cinnamon—Kerneel
nutmeg—Muschotnät

ginger—Enjwa
star anise—Stearn-aniess
saffron—Safran
summer savory—Päpakrut
dill—Dell
bay leaf—Luabäa Blaut

FOODS

food—Äte
bread (brown)—Broot
bread (white)—Bultje
bun—Tweeback
biscuit—Schnetje
peppernut—Papanät
butter—Botta
meat—Fleesch
pork—Schwienfleesch
bacon—Spakj
cracklings—Jreewe
sausage—Worscht
beef—Rintfleesch
chicken—Heenafleesch
fruit stuffing—Bobbat

fish—Fesch
cheese—Kjees
cottage cheese—Gloms
perogies—Wrennetje
noodles—Kjieltje
egg—Ei
soup—Supp
borscht—Borscht
moes—Mooss (e.g., Plume Mooss)
oatmeal (porridge)—Howajrett
pot barley—Joaschtnejrett
fritter, cookie—Kook/Kuak
New Year's fritter—Portseltje
pudding—Pudding
pie—Pei

DRINKS

drink—Drunk
water—Wota
coffee—Koffe
tea—Tee
homemade postum—Prips
milk—Malkj

cream—Schmaunt
buttermilk—Bottamalkj
wine—Wien
brandy—Braunwien
beer—Beea

GARDEN VEGETABLES

vegetable—Jemies
cabbage—Komst
potato—Eadschock
sunflower—Knacksot
bean—Schaubel
pea—Oaft
corn—Korn, Kuckerus
onion—(T)sippel
parsnip—Postanack
parsley—Peetaselj
turnip—Wruck

summer turnip—Wrieb
beet—Beet
carrot—Jalmäa
radish—Radiestje
cucumber—Gurkj
watermelon—Rebus, Arbus
muskmelon—Meloon
pumpkin—Kjarps
tomato—Bockelzhonn
lettuce—(T)selot

ORCHARD FRUIT	fruit—Frucht	orange—Aupel(t)sien
	mulberry—Mulbäa	lemon—(T)sitroon
	plum—Plum	strawberry—Eadbäa
	raisin—Rasien	raspberry—Hinnbäa, Himmbäa
	currant—Olbassem	saskatoon berry—Junibäa
	gooseberry—Kjressbäa	cranberry—Suabäa
	pear—Bäa	chokecherry—schwoate, kjrasche, or strufe Kjoasch
	apple—Aupel	
	apricot—Aupelkoos	pincherry—roode Kjoasch

CROPS	grain—Jeträjd	barley—Joascht
	seed—Sot	rye—Rogg
	wheat—Weit	flax—Flauss
	oats—Howa	hay—Hei

FARM ANIMALS	cattle—Fee	sheep—Schop
	cow—Koo	lamb—Laum
	bull—Boll	goose—Gauns
	ox—Oss	gander—Gaunta
	calf—Kaulf	goslings—Janstjes
	horse—Peat	duck—Ent
	mare—Kobbel	drake—Woat
	stallion—Hinkjst	Hen—Han
	gelding—Kunta	rooster—Hon
	colt—Falm	chick—Kjikjel
	pig—Schwien	peacock—Pauhon
	sow—Sääj	dog—Hunt
	boar—Kujel	cat—Kaut
	piglet—Foakjel	tomcat—Kota
	billy goat—Kosebock	

FARM IMPLEMENTS	implement—Jreetschoft	threshing machine—Draschmaschien
	plow—Plooch/Pluach	spade—Spodem
	disc—Soodeschnieda	shovel—Scheffel
	harrow—Äajd	rake—Hoakj
	drill—Drill	pitchfork—Forkj
	mower—Graussmaschien	hoe—Hack
	scythe—Sans(s)	Dutch hoe—Schuwa
	binder—Binja	postmaul—Passäkjel
	tractor—Treckta	crowbar—Koofoot
	packer—Waults, Packa	

TOOLS

hammer—Homa	pliers—Tang
saw—Soag	file—Fiel
ruler—Motstock	rasp—Rausp
plane—Häwel	hatchet—Biel
drill—Boa	axe—Akjs
screwdriver—Schruwedreia	chisel—Beitel

MISCELLANEOUS OBJECTS

wood—Holt	broom—Bassem
coal—Kole	book—Book/Buak
kerosene—Kjersien	ball—Baul
oil—Eelj	needle—Notel
box—Doos	thread—Twearm, Drot

CONVEYANCES

conveyance—Foatijch	bobsleigh—groota Schläde
buggy—Bogge	cutter—kjliena Schläde
sulky—(T)solkje	stoneboat—Mest-schläde
wagon—Woage	boat—Kon
hayrack—Heirekj	ferry—Prom
wheelbarrow—Mestkoa	ship—Schepp
car—Koa	

CLOTHING

clothing—Kjleeda	pants—Bekjse
hat—Hoot	suspenders—Droagbenja
cap—Mets	underwear—Unjakjleeda
coat—Äwarock	shirt—Hamd
fur coat—Pels	tie—Schlips
jacket—Waums	sweater—Swetta
gloves—Finjahaunschtje	dress—Kjleet
mitts—Fusthaunschtje	belt (woman's)—Lief-baunt
boot—Steewel	blouse—Blus
shoe—Schoo	skirt—Rock
shoelace—Schoobaunt	apron—Schaldook/Schalduak
stocking—Stremp	

OUTDOORS

outdoors—Bute	earth (ground)—Ead
sun—Sonn	air—Loft
moon—Mon	wind—Wint
star—Stearn	sky—Himmel
world—Welt	cloud—Wolkj
land—Launt	thundercloud—Schwoakj
hill—Boajch, Boaj	thunder—Rummel
valley—Hollinj, Dol	lightning—Blits
ocean—Mäa	storm—Storm
lake—See	rain—Räajen
river—Fluss	hail—Hoagel
slough—Schluw	ice—Iess
field—Stap	snow—Schnee
stone—Steen	sunshine—Sonneschien
road—Wajch	

PLANTLIFE

plant—Plaunt	root—Wartel
grass—Grauss	branch—Aust
weed—Onnkrut	leaf—Blaut
flower—Bloom	oak—Äkj
rose—Roos	birch—Boakj
tulip—Tulp	poplar—Papel
everlasting—Stroobloom	spruce—Dauneboom
Pansy—Schwaulm-oogtje/	willow—Wied
-uagtje	brush—Struck
crocus—Pelsbloom	bush—Bosch
tree—Boom	forest—Wolt
trunk—Staum	

WILD MAMMALS

animal—Tia	rabbit—Hos
mouse—Mus	badger—Daks
gopher—Stapmus	fox—Foss
weasel—Wäsel	wolf—Wulf
rat—Raut	deer—Hersch
muskrat—Muschelraut	bear—Boa
skunk—Stinkjkaut	

OTHER ANIMALS

turtle—Schiltkjrät
snake—Schlang
toad—Kjrät
frog—Pogg
salamander—Ead-salmaunda
fish—Fesch
sturgeon—Stäa
pike—Häakjt
burbot—Kwaup

goldeye—Plauta
chub—Runda
sucker—(T)socka
butterfly—Flotta
bumblebee—Biehommel
fly—Fläj
bluebottle fly—Modeschieta
mosquito—Migj
grasshopper—Grausshoppa

WILD BIRDS

bird—Foagel
sparrow—Spoalinkj
swallow—Schwaulm
blackbird—Spree
meadowlark—Jung-febiela
robin—Rootbuck
woodpecker—Holthacka
cuckoo—Kuckuck
killdeer—Katrien
dove—Duw
goose—Gauns

prairie chicken—Staphan
gull—Meew
crow—Krauj
hawk—Hoftje
owl—Ul
eagle—Odla
swan—Schwon
crane—Krauntje
stork—Storch
duck—Ent

COLORS

color—Kolleea
blue—blauw
red—root
yellow—jäl
orange—dunkel jäl
green—jreen

purple—fieoletteblauw
pink—fleischfoawijch
brown—brun
black—schwoat
gray—grauw
white—witt

TIME

time—Tiet
second—Sekund
minute—Minut
hour—Stund
(of the) morning—(t)semorjens
afternoon—nomeddach
twilight—Tweediesta
evening—Owent
night—Nacht
day—Dach

today—fonndoag
yesterday—jistre
tomorrow—morje
week—Wäakj
month—Moonat
spring—Farjoa
summer—Somma
fall—Hoafst
winter—Winta
year—Joa

Days

Monday—Mondach
Tuesday—Dinjsdach
Wednesday—Meddwääkj
Thursday—Donnadach

Friday—Friedach
Saturday—Sinnowent
Sunday—Sinndach

Months

January—Jaunuoa
February—Feebruoa
March—Moats
April—Aprell
May—Mei
June—Junie

July—Julie
August—August, Aust
September—Septamba
October—Oktooba
November—Nowamba
December—Dee(t)samba

Cardinal Numbers

number—Numma
zero—null
one—eent*
two—twee
three—dree
four—feea
five—fiew
six—sass
seven—säwen
eight—acht
nine—näajen
ten—tian
eleven—alw

twelve—twalw
thirteen—drettian
fourteen—featian
fifteen—feftian
twenty—twintijch
twenty-one—een-enn-twintijch
thirty—dartijch
forty—featijch
fifty—feftijch
hundred—hundat
thousand—dusent
million—millijoon

*Note use as adj.: *een* (masc., neut.), *eene* (fem.).

Ordinal Numbers*

first—eascht-
second—tweed-
third—dredd-
fourth—fead-
fifth—feft-
sixth—sasst-
seventh—säwend-
eighth—acht-
ninth—näajend-
tenth—tiand-

eleventh—alft-
twelfth—twalft-
thirteenth—drettiand-
fourteenth—featiand-
fifteenth—feftiand-
twentieth—twintijchst-
hundredth—hundatst-
thousandth—dusentst-
millionth—millijoonst-

*Note that ordinal numbers take adjectival endings.

SOME COGNATE WORDS

Plautdietsch Word	Meaning	Cognate English Word
Baunt	(string)	band
blank	(shiny)	blank
Blaut	(leaf)	blade
Boom	(tree)	beam
Dakj	(cover)	deck
Desch	(table)	desk
Faspa	(coffee break)	vesper
Faut	(crock)	vat
foare	(to drive)	fare (i.e., to fare forth)
groot	(big)	great
Hoafst	(autumn)	harvest
Holt	(wood)	holt
Hunt	(dog)	hound
jäat	(ferments)	yeast
Jacht	(hunt)	yacht
jripp	(catch)	grip
Kjnajcht	(hired man)	knight
Kruck	(jug)	crock
Meddach	(dinner)	mid-day
Mäl	(flour)	meal (e.g., cornmeal)
Oog	(eye)	ogle
Owe	(stove)	oven
Päakjel	(brine)	pickle
piepe	(to whistle)	pipe
Plot	(baking pan)	plate
Rigje	(back, backbone)	ridge
schlo	(strike)	slay
schmakje	(to taste)	smack (i.e., of one's lips)
schmaul	(narrow)	small
spaun	(hitch)	span
Stap	(field)	steppe
Staul	(barn)	stall
stoawe	(to die)	starve
Stool	(chair)	stool
Strank	(rope)	string
tale	(to count)	tell (cf. bank teller)
Tint	(ink)	tint
Topp	(pot)	tub
wada	(again)	further
sup	(guzzle)	sip

FURTHER READING

This list, it is hoped, is representative of the rapidly growing wealth of material pertaining to Mennonite studies. The selection is based on those subjects pertinent to this book. Some of the materials themselves—for example, C. Henry Smith, *The Story of the Mennonites*, 1981, and Julius G. Toews and Lawrence Klippenstein, eds., *Manitoba Mennonite Memories*, 1974—have lengthy bibliographies, and the reader is referred to them for still further reading, if desired.

The list has been divided into three sections. The reader should be aware that a few works, although listed but once, might well fit under more than one category.

HISTORICAL/CRITICAL STUDIES

Beedel, Suzanne. *Windmills*. Vancouver: David and Charles, 1975.

Bender, Harold S. *Mennonites and Their Heritage: Mennonite Origins in Europe*. Akron, Pa.: Mennonite Central Committee, 1942.

Doell, Leonard. *The Bergthaler Mennonite Church of Saskatchewan 1892–1975*. Winnipeg: CMBC Publications, 1987.

Dyck, Cornelius J., ed. *An Introduction to Mennonite History*. Scottdale, Pa.: Herald Press, 1981.

——. *A Legacy of Faith: The Heritage of Menno Simons*. Newton, Kans.: Faith and Life Press, 1962.

Epp, David H. *Johann Cornies*. Rosthern, Sask.: Echo Verlag, 1946.

Epp, Frank H. *Education with a Plus: The Story of Rosthern Junior College*. Waterloo, Ont.: Conrad Press, 1975.

——. *Mennonite Exodus: The Rescue and Re-settlement of the Russian Mennonites Since the Russian Revolution*. Altona, Man.: D. W. Friesen and Sons, 1962.

——. *Mennonites in Canada, 1786–1920: The History of a Separate People*. Toronto: Macmillan of Canada, 1974.

——. *Mennonites in Canada, 1920–1940: A People's Struggle for Survival*. Toronto: Macmillan of Canada, 1982.

Francis, E. K. *In Search of Utopia: The Mennonites in Manitoba*. Altona, Man.: D. W. Friesen and Sons, 1955.

Friesen, George P. *Fangs of Bolshevism: or, Friesen-Braun Trials in Saskatchewan, 1924–29*. Saskatoon: n.p., 1930.

Friesen, I. I. "The Mennonites in Western Canada with Special Reference to Education" (unpublished M.A. thesis). University of Saskatchewan, Saskatoon, 1934.

Friesen, John. *Mennonites Through the Centuries: From the Netherlands to Canada*. Steinbach, Man.: Mennonite Village Museum, 1985.

Friesen, Peter M. *The Mennonite Brotherhood in Russia (1789–1910)*, trans. J. B. Toews and others. Fresno, Calif.: Board of Christian Literature, 1978.

Gleysteen, Jan. *Mennonite Tourguide of Western Europe*. Scottdale, Pa.: Herald Press, 1984.

Goerz, H. *Die Molotschnaen Ansiedlung: Enstehung, Entwicklung und Untergang*. Steinbach, Man.: Echo Verlag, 1951.

Haak, Bob. *The Golden Age: Dutch Painters of the Seventeenth Century*, trans. and ed. Elizabeth Willems-Treeman. London: Thames and Hudson, 1984.

Hiebert, P. C., and Orie O. Miller, eds. *Feeding the Hungry: Russia Famine 1919–1925*. Scottdale, Pa.: Mennonite Central Committee, 1929.

Horsch, John. *Mennonites in Europe*. Scottdale, Pa.: Herald Press, 1950.

Klippenstein, Lawrence. *David Klassen and the Mennonites*. Agincourt, Ont.: Book Society of Canada, 1982.

——. *That There Be Peace: Mennonites in Canada and World War II*. Winnipeg: Manitoba CO Reunion Committee, 1979.

Klippenstein, Lawrence, and Peter Goertzen, eds. *Mennonite Village Museum*. Steinbach, Man.: Manitoba Village Museum, 1984.

Krahn, Cornelius J. *Dutch Anabaptism: Origin, Spread, Life and Thought (1450–1600)*. The Hague: Martinus Nijhoff, 1968.

Loewen, Harry, ed. *Mennonite Images: Historical, Cultural, and Literary Essays Dealing with Mennonite Issues*. Winnipeg: Hyperion Press, 1980.

Loewen, Harry, and Al Reimer, eds. *Visions and Realities: Essays, Poems, and Fiction Dealing with Mennonite Issues*. Winnipeg: Hyperion Press, 1985.

Lohrenz, Gerhard. *Heritage Remembered: A Pictorial Survey of Mennonites in Prussia and Russia*. Winnipeg: CMBC Publications, 1974.

———. *The Mennonites of Western Canada*. Winnipeg: n.p., 1974.

The Mennonite Encyclopedia, 4 vols. Scottdale, Pa.: Mennonite Publishing House, 1955–59.

Neudorf, Johann J., Heinrich J. Neudorf, and David D. Rempel, eds. *Osterwick, 1812–1943*. Clearbrook, B.C.: A. Olfert and Sons, 1972.

Peters, Victor. *Nestor Makhno, The Life of an Anarchist*. Winnipeg: Echo Books, 1970.

Poettcker, Henry, and Rudy A. Regehr, eds. *Call to Faithfulness: Essays in Canadian Mennonite Studies*. Winnipeg: Canadian Mennonite Bible College, 1972.

Quiring, Walter, and Helen Bartel. *In the Fullness of Time, 150 Years of Mennonite Sojourn in Russia*, trans. Katherine Janzen. Waterloo, Ont.: Reeve Bean, 1974.

———. *Mennonites in Canada: A Pictorial Review*. Altona, Man.: D. W. Friesen and Sons, 1961.

Redekop, Calvin Wall. *The Old Colony Mennonites: Dilemmas of Ethnic Minority Life*. Baltimore: John Hopkins Press, 1969.

Sawatzky, Harry Leonard. *They Sought a Country: Mennonite Colonization in Mexico*. Berkeley: University of California, 1971.

Schroeder, William. *The Bergthal Colony*. Winnipeg: CMBC Publications, 1974.

Simons, Menno. *The Complete Writings of Menno Simons*, trans. Leonard Verduin, ed. John Christian Wenger, with a biography by Harold S. Bender. Scottdale, Pa.: Herald Press, 1956.

Smith, C. Henry. *Mennonites and Their Heritage: Mennonites in America*. Akron, Pa.: Mennonite Central Committee, 1942.

———. *The Story of the Mennonites*, 5th edn., rev. Cornelius Krahn. Newton, Kans.: Faith and Life Press, 1981.

Stockhuyzen, Frederick. *The Dutch Windmill*. London: Merlin Press, 1962.

Sudermann, Leonhard. *In Search of Freedom*, trans. Elmer F. Suderman. Steinbach, Man.: Derksen Printers, 1974.

Unruh, Abe J. *The Helpless Poles*. Newton, Kans.: Mennonite Library and Archives, 1973.

Unruh, John C. *In the Name of Christ: A History of the Mennonite Central Committee and Its Service, 1920–1951*. Scottdale, Pa.: Herald Press, 1952.

Van Braght, Thieleman J. *The Bloody Theater or Martyrs Mirror*, trans. Joseph F. Sohm from the 1660 edn. Scottdale, Pa.: Herald Press, 1975.

Language/Folklore Studies

Bastide, J. A. Jockin-la, and G. van Kooten. *Cassell's English-Dutch, Dutch-English Dictionary*. London: Cassell, 1981.

Bett, Henry. *Nursery Rhymes and Tales: Their Origin and History*. London: Methuen, 1924.

Betteridge, Harold T., ed. *Cassell's German and English Dictionary* (based on edn. by Karl Breul). London: Cassell, 1957.

Brednich, Rolf Wilhelm. *Mennonite Folklife and Folklore: A Preliminary Report* (National Museum of Man Mercury Series; Canadian Centre for Folk Culture Studies, Paper No. 22). Ottawa: National Museums of Canada, 1977.

Commins, Dorothy Berliner. *Lullabies of Many Lands*. New York: Harper, 1941.

Davis, Norman. *Sweet's Anglo-Saxon Primer*. Oxford: Clarendon Press, 1953.

Dutton-Smith, Brian. *The Folkgames of Children*. Austin: University of Texas Press, 1972.

Dyck, Henry Dietrich. "Language Differentiation in Two Low German Groups in Canada" (unpublished Ph.D. dissertation). University of Pennsylvania, Philadelphia, 1964.

Flint Board of Education. *Ring a Ring O'Roses: Stories, Games and Finger Plays for Pre-School Children*. Flint, Mich.: Flint Public Library, 1981.

Fowke, Edith. *Folklore of Canada*. Toronto: McClelland and Stewart, 1976.

Friesen, J. John. "Romance of Low German," *Mennonite Life* II (April, 1947), 22–23, 47.

Goerzen, J. W. *Low German in Canada: A Study of "Plautdietsch" as Spoken by the Mennonite Immigrants from Russia*. Edmonton; n.p., 1970.

————. "'Plautdietsch' and English," *Mennonite Life* VII (January, 1952), 18–19.

Hall, John R. Clark. *A Concise Anglo-Saxon Dictionary*. Cambridge: University Press, 1966.

Klassen, Doreen. *Singing Mennonite: Low German Songs among the Mennonites*. Winnipeg: University of Manitoba Press, 1988.

Kliewer, Warren. "Collecting Folklore among Mennonites," *Mennonite Life* XVI, (July, 1961), 109–12.

————. "Low German Children's Rimes," *Mennonite Life* XIV (July, 1959), 141–42.

————. "Low German Proverbs," *Mennonite Life* XV (April, 1960), 77–80.

————. "More Low German Children's Rhymes," *Mennonite Life* XV (October, 1960), 173–74, 180.

Koolhoven, H. *Teach Yourself Dutch*. London: English Universities Press, 1961.

Krahn, Cornelius. "Mennonite Plautdietsch," *Mennonite Quarterly Review* XXX (July, 1959), 256–59.

Meyer, Erika. *Elementary German*. Boston: Houghton Mifflin, 1954.

Mother Goose. *The Annotated Mother Goose: Nursery Rhymes Old and New*, arr. William S. Baring-Gould and Ceil Baring-Gould. New York: Clarkson N. Potter, 1962.

Mountain Lake Gopher Historians, Chapter II. *Off the Mountain Lake Range: A Collection of Old Recipes and Customs Brought to This Country by the Early Settlers of This Community*. Mountain Lake, Minn.: Mountain Lake Gopher Historians, Chapter II, 1958.

Opie, Iona, and Peter Opie. *The Lore and Language of School Children*. Oxford: Clarendon Press, 1959.

Peacock, Kenneth. *Twenty Ethnic Songs from Western Canada* (National Museums of Canada Bulletin No. 211, Anthropological Series No. 76). Ottawa: Queen's Printer, 1966.

Reimer, Al. "There's now an 'official' way to write Low German," *Mennonite Mirror* XI (June, 1982), 7–8.

Reimer, Anne. "Towards an Orthography of Low German" (course essay, German Department), University of Winnipeg, 1981.

Rempel, Herman. *Kjenn Jie Noch Plautdietsch? A Mennonite Low German Dictionary*. Winnipeg: Mennonite Literary Society, 1984.

Stevenson, Burton. *The Home Book of Proverbs, Maxims and Familiar Phrases*. New York: Macmillan, 1948.

Thiessen, Jack. "The Low Geman of the Canadian Mennonites," *Mennonite Life* XXII (July, 1967), 110–16.

————. *Mennonite Low German Dictionary*. Marburg: N. G. Elwert, 1977.

————. "Mennonite *Plautdietsch*—The Odyssey of a People." Forthcoming.

————. "A New Look at an Old Problem: Mennonite *Plautdietsch*." Forthcoming.

Wiens, Gerhard. "Russian in Low German," *Mennonite Life* XIII (April, 1958), 75–78.

Withers, Carl, and Sula Benet. *Riddles of Many Lands*. New York: Abelard-Schuman, 1956.

AUTOBIOGRAPHICAL/LITERARY WORKS

Dyck, Arnold. *Koop enn Bua opp Reise . . .* (Collected Works of Arnold Dyck, Vol. II), ed. Al Reimer. Winnipeg: Manitoba Mennonite Historical Society, 1986.

————. *Lost in the Steppes*, trans. Henry D. Dyck. Steinbach, Man.: Derksen Printers, 1974.

Epp, George K., and others, eds. *Harvest: Anthology of Mennonite Writing in Canada, 1874–1974*. Winnipeg: Centennial Committee of the Mennonite Historical Society of Manitoba, 1974.

Epp, Margaret. *The Earth Is Round*. Winnipeg: Christian Press, 1974.

————. *A Fountain Sealed*. Grand Rapids, Mich.: Zondervan, 1965.

Epp, Peter G. *Agatchen, A Russian Mennonite Mother's Story*, trans. and ed. Peter Pauls, Winnipeg: Hyperion Press, 1986.

Epp, Reuben. *Biem Aunsiedle* (record of *Plautdietsch* stories and humor). Winnipeg: R.E.C. Recordings, 1972.

————. *Onse Lied Vetahle* (record of *Plautdietsch* stories and verse). Winnipeg: R.E.C. Recordings, 1973.

————. *Plautdietsche Schreftsteckja*. Steinbach, Man.: Derksen Printers, 1972.

Friesen, Anna, and Victor Carl Friesen. *The Mulberry Tree*. Winnipeg: Queenston House, 1985.

Friesen, Patrick. *The Shunning*. Winnipeg: Turnstone Press, 1980.

Goulden (Unger), Veleda. *De Goldene Schlut: A Coloring Book and Collection of Low German Nursery Rhymes*. Steinbach, Man.: Derksen Printers, 1974.

Harder, Hans. *No Strangers in Exile.*, trans., ed., and expand. Al Reimer. Winnipeg: Hyperion Press, 1979.

Heischraitje & Willa Honich (Locusts and Wild Honey). *Ditt Sied—Jant Sied* (record of *Plautdietsch* songs). Landmark, Man.: Knackzote Records, 1982.

———. *Sprie* (record of *Plautdietsch* songs). Landmark, Man.: Knackzote Records, 1980.

Hiebert, Paul. *Doubting Castle*. Winnipeg: Queenston House, 1976.

Lohrenz, Gerhard. *Storm Tossed: The Personal Story of a Canadian Mennonite from Russia*. Winnipeg: Christian Press, 1976.

Martens, Wilfred. *River of Glass*. Scottdale, Pa: Herald Press, 1980.

Neufeld, Dietrich. *A Russian Dance of Death*, trans. and ed. Al Reimer. Winnipeg: Hyperion Press, 1977.

Peters, Elisabeth. *Dee Tjoaschenhatj (The Cherryhedge)*. Steinbach, Man.: Derksen Printers, 1984.

Reimer, Al. *My Harp Is Turned to Mourning*. Winnipeg: Hyperion Press, 1985.

Reimer, Al, Anne Reimer, and Jack Thiessen, eds. *A Sackful of Plautdietsch*. Winnipeg: Hyperion Press, 1983.

Rimland, Ingrid. *The Wanderers: The Saga of Three Women Who Survived*. St. Louis: Concordia Publishing House, 1977.

Senn, Fritz (Gerhard Friesen). *Das Dorf in Abendgrauen*, ed. Elisabeth Peters. Winnipeg: Verein zur Plege der Deutschen Sprache, 1974.

———. *Gesammalte Gedichte and Prosa*, ed. Victor G. Doerksen. Winnipeg: CMBC Publications, 1987.

Smucker, Barbara Claassen. *Days of Terror*. Toronto: Clarke Irwin, 1979.

Toews, Julius G., and Lawrence Klippenstein, eds. *Manitoba Mennonite Memories*. Altona and Steinbach: Manitoba Mennonite Centennial Committee, 1974.

Waltner-Toews, David. *Good Housekeeping*. Winnipeg: Turnstone Press, 1983.

Wiebe, Rudy. *The Blue Mountains of China*. Toronto: McClelland and Stewart, 1970.

———. *Peace Shall Destroy Many*. Toronto: McClelland and Stewart, 1962.

INDEX TO FIRST LINES
(OF RHYMING ITEMS)

The figures in parentheses refer to the chapter and item number.

PLAUTDIETSCH

Äkje, bäkje, Boakjeholt (8-3)
Aprell (13-9)
Aule leewe Janstjes, komt no mie (8-8)
Aun Gottes säajen (13-11)
Aunn, spaun aun (6-25)

Backe, backe, Kooke (7-18)
Benjeltje, ke-penjeltje (6-9)
Best mie goot (6-11)
Blinje Koo, ekj leid die (8-7)
Botta, Botta (6-3)

Daut deat en Stoot (14-47)
Daut räajent (13-12)
Daut's en Wada-profeet (13-10)
De Brigj dee ess jebroake (8-11)
De easchte Dach en Gaust (14-11)
De Kjäakjsche enn de Kaut (12-9)
De Kosebock sprinjt oppem Boajch (6-28)
De Mensch denkjt (14-27)
De Wausch henjt oppem Tun (5-6)
Derkj Dycke Derkj drooch (10-10)
Doa flooch en Foagel stoakj (10-2)
Doa kome twee jegone (7-16)
Dume, schedde Plume (7-12)

Eadbäa, Eadbäa (5-3)
Eascht Mumm (6-14)
Eene, meene, mekje (T)soagel (8-4)

Eene woat oolt auss ne Koo (14-14)
Eent flooch oost (11-25)
Eent, twee, dree (7-15)
Eent, twee, dree, feea (6-12)
Ekj ät waut goa ess (14-32)
Ekj enn du (8-2)
Ekj enn du enn dee (7-14)
Ekj jinkj emol nom Woolt (9-4)
Ekj kjeem aun jerant (6-5)
Ekj kjeem fomm Boajch jerant (6-6)
Ekj saj die woa (10-7)
Ekj weet waut niess (6-29)
Ekj wensch, ekj wensch (6-7)
En Droom ess en Droch (14-36)
En grootet Jeschrejcht (14-35)
En "muss" ess en Schwank (11-22)
En scheena gooda Owent enn eene schaftje Tiet (9-5)

Fäl Henj (12-18)
Fäl Jast (12-7)
Fesch enn (T)selot (12-2)
Fespräakje ess "ehrlich" (15-29)
Fia moake, Kjieltje koake (7-1)
Flekj opp' Loch (11-1)
Fomm Schusta no Hus (6-21)
Fonn fäare—uj, uj! (12-13)
Fonn Hoate enn Jenode (14-10)

Gooda-morje, one sorje! (10-5)

Haj, du lostijch (8-1)
Haj, soo ritt dee Harschoft (7-11)
Hauns mett de Fiddel (6-30)
Hauns Ullarijch (6-17)
Hooch henjt Hendrikj (10-1)

Hupps, hupps, hupps, hupps, seedatje (7-8)
Hupps, Kunta, riede (7-10)
Hupptje, Mauntje, riede (7-9)

Iesaak, Spriesack (6-23)

Jeat, schmeat (6-24)
Jelt, Jelt (14-22)
Johaun, spaun aun (6-26)
Jreen enn root (12-11)
Jriepa, Piepa [I] (8-5)
Jriepa, Piepa [II] (8-6)

Kjemt Tiet, kjemt Rot (13-16)
Kjenntje, Multje (7-2)
Kjleeda moake Lied (12-14)
Kjliena Finja (7-13)
Kjlinja-maun enn Klaupa-maun (10-3)
Kjrei-a-rie (7-3)
Komm wan du west, dan komm (9-2)
Komm, wie welle waundre (8-9)
Kromm, eromm (5-2)

Langet Drot (12-17)
Laumtje haud en Kobbeltje (6-27)
Lea, lea, Lommtopp (6-31)
Lott ess doot, Lott ess doot (9-3)

Mama, Papa, Aupel, Bäa (6-10)
Marie, Marie, maruschtje (5-4)
Mejchel, prejchel, lot mie läwe (6-18)
Mett däm Hoot enne Haunt (15-24)
Mie hungat (6-13)
Mitsch, Pitsch, Päpa-mäl (6-16)
Morje-stund (13-7)
Mutta doot (11-3)

O jana jo (14-18)
Oost, wast (12-19)
Owent—root (13-6)

Peeta enn Peewel jinje hauwe (6-22)
Peeta, Peeta, komm mol äte (5-1)

Rea, rea, Jrettje (7-17)
Runde, runde, Roosekrauns (8-10)
Ruzhe, Petruzhe (6-19)

Saj, saj wada (6-8)
Schlop, Kjintje, schlop (6-2)
Schockel, Schockel, scheia (7-5)
Schusta, Schusta, schnurr (6-20)
Sie stell (6-15)
Sinj'm [sinj too am], sinj'm, sinj'm, soo
   (9-1)
Somma, audee (13-14)
Soo jeit et oppe Welt (14-6)
Spoa enne Noot (14-31)
Sprinj, Bockje, sprinj (7-6)
Straum oppe Strot (12-12)
Stripp, stripp, stroll (6-1)

Troch, Troch, treitje (7-7)

Wää daut kjliene nijch eat (15-49)
Wää nijch too Tiet toom äte kjemt (12-
   6)
Wää well scheene Kooke backe (6-4)
Wan eene eenmol lijcht (15-30)
Wan en Hon kjreit (13-1)
Wan et emm Winta kracht (13-8)
Wellem, kjnell'm (7-4)
Wie senn kjliene Schnetje (7-19)
Wie witte Wiewa welle witte Winjle
   wausche (10-9)
Woo soll et woare? (5-5)

ENGLISH

A dream is as naught (14-36)
A duty is a command (11-22)
A great big to-do (14-35)
All beloved goslings, come to me (8-8)
Ann, hitch the team (6-25)
April (13-9)

Baking, baking, cookies (7-18)
Be still (6-15)
Butter, butter (6-3)

Clothes now make the man (12-14)
Come if you will, then come (9-2)
Come, we want to wander (8-9)
Crow-a-rie (7-3)

Early morn (13-7)
East, west (12-19)
Eenie, meenie, donkey's tail (8-4)
Evening—red (13-6)

First aunt (6-14)
For one's heartfelt compassion (14-10)
From in front—my, my! (12-13)
From shoester let's run (6-21)

Georgie, peorgie (6-24)
Gold, gold (14-22)
Good evening this New Year's, good
   times to all of you (9-5)
Good-morrow, without sorrow! (10-5)

Hans Slim-n-Trim (6-17)
Hans with the fiddle (6-30)
Heigh, so rides the gentry (7-11)
Hop, hop, hop, hop, hop away (7-8)
Hopalong, little man, ride away (7-9)
How will it all end? (5-5)

I came a-running down (6-6)
I came running here (6-5)
I eat what is here (14-32)
I once went to the woods (9-4)
I say with care (10-7)
I wish, I plan (6-7)
If you me love (6-11)
I'm hungry (6-13)
In time come needs (13-16)
Isaak, sprisaak (6-23)
It takes a while (14-47)
It's raining (13-12)

Jingle-man and clatter-man (10-3)
Jump, billy goat, jump (7-6)

Krum, e-rum (5-2)

Lambkin had a little mare (6-27)
Learn, learn, lum-dumb (6-31)
Lettuce and fish (12-2)
Little finger (7-13)
Long stitch (12-17)
Lope, horsey, lope (7-10)
Lot is dead, Lot is dead (9-3)

Make the fire, cook the noodles (7-1)
Mamma, Papa, apple, pear (6-10)
Man proposes (14-27)
Many a guest (12-7)
Many a hand (12-18)
Marie, Marie, *maruschtje* (5-4)
Michael, pichael, let me live (6-18)
Mitch, pitch, pepper mill (6-16)
Mother—dead (11-3)

Now, John, hitch up (6-26)

O yessiree (14-18)
Oak and boak and birch-tree wood (8-3)
Old blind cow, I lead you (8-7)
On God's good tending (13-11)
On the wall—tick-tock (10-1)
One Dirk Dyck's Dirk toted (10-10)
One flew east (11-25)
One gets as old as a cow (14-14)
One, two, three (7-15)
One, two, three, four (6-12)

Patch-on-skirt (11-1)
Peter and Paul both went a-mowing (6-
   22)
Peter, Peter, time for eating (5-1)
Pretty up town (12-12)

Red and green (12-11)
Round and round the rosy crown (8-10)
Ruzhe, Petruzhe (6-19)

Say, say, say it (6-8)
She who cookies wants to bake (6-4)
Shoester, shoester, shoe (6-20)
Shuckle, shuckle, shia (7-5)
Singing, singing, singing, Hi! (9-1)
Sleep, wee one, sleep (6-2)
So things are in the world (14-6)
Spare when in need (14-31)